JOYFUL AND HEALTHY LIVING

DR. V. P. GUPTA

NewDelhi • London

BLUEROSE PUBLISHERS
India | U.K.

Copyright © Dr. V. P. Gupta 2024

All rights reserved by author. No part of this publication may be reproduced, stored in a retrieval system or transmitted in any form or by any means, electronic, mechanical, photocopying, recording or otherwise, without the prior permission of the author. Although every precaution has been taken to verify the accuracy of the information contained herein, the publisher assume no responsibility for any errors or omissions. No liability is assumed for damages that may result from the use of information contained within.

BlueRose Publishers takes no responsibility for any damages, losses, or liabilities that may arise from the use or misuse of the information, products, or services provided in this publication.

For permissions requests or inquiries regarding this publication, please contact:

BLUEROSE PUBLISHERS
www.BlueRoseONE.com
info@bluerosepublishers.com
+91 8882 898 898
+4407342408967

ISBN: 978-93-6783-244-8

Cover design: Daksh
Typesetting: Tanya Raj Upadhyay

First Edition: November 2024

Dedicated to My Loving and visionary Parents

&

Family Members

Dr. V. P. Gupta

M.Sc. Ph. D. (Chemistry), EPPAM Manchester

Formerly Prof. of Chemistry in NCERT (India)

&

World Bank Team Member (DPEP Project)

Editor

ARYAN GUPTA B.S.

University of California Berkeley (UCB)

PREFACE

The world population reached 8,118,835,999 by March, 2024 scattered over different continents, differing in their culture, customs, religions, language and socio - economic diversities. If the United States of America can boast of world's largest economy, followed by China, Germany, India and Japan, but South Sudan, Burundi, Central African Republic, Democratic Republic of the Congo fall in line of the poorest countries of the world, lingering much behind with a GDP-PPP of $476, 890, 1109 and $1579. Americans are highly effluent people, but are known for innovations with maximum Nobel prize winners. The American Universities are the most sought seats of learning by youths all over the globe. It's like a dream come true for anyone who gets admitted to any university in America. India is a very developing Nation with more than750 medical colleges, 1,113 Central or State universities, 3,596 privately owned, 4500 engineering colleges and 43,796 other colleges. According to the Ministry of External Affairs report, there are 29M NRIs and PIOs (including OCIs) residing outside India.

Foreign Indians comprise the world's largest overseas Diaspora with about 2.5 M Indians migrating overseas every year. 58,000 Indians got American citizenship in 2023. India is now considered as one of the strongest military powers, but we are a peace loving Nation unlike many other countries. Russia, a super power, is entangled in war with a very small country like Ukraine for the last two years and is killing thousands of innocent peace loving people. Such an administration where there is no freedom to speak and not allowed to criticize the government is just unacceptable to peace loving people of any country.

Israel is another country, who has been attacking residents of Palestine and has killed more than 40,000 innocent civilians on the pretext of teaching a lesson to terrorists of Hamas since October, 2023. May be true to some extent but there is no fault of innocent children and expecting mothers. After all, why is this happening in the world? India is known for unity in diversity with the highest population of 1,400,000,000 in the world, people speaking different languages and following different religions but all stand as one united Nation. India has never attacked any neighboring countries, rather helped people of earlier East Pakistan to get rid of the cruel army of West Pakistan and got them freedom as an Independent Nation named as Bangladesh in 1971.

Leading a joyful and healthy life involves an amalgamation of physical, mental and emotional well - being. Various attributes like gratitude to all, passion for work, love for nation, care of nature, caring and sharing with friends around us and the needy ones, self discipline in terms of food habits, exercises, adequate sleep, away from worries and tensions, regular visits to family members, relatives and friends, off and on excursions with family, positive thinking, and continuous learning and a few more as needed to help us to remain joyful and healthy. All such attributes are discussed in detail in the present book.

Most of the Indians living in rural areas and scattered huts are the happiest lot believing in their own religion and living as big families with extra harmony with people of other faith around them. This may be true in small towns of India and many other developing and developed countries and cities. However, residents of cosmopolitan cities are affected by other cultures, where we come across self centered persons living in high societies. But even then on the whole, most Indians are leading a joyful and healthy life and so may be the case in many other countries. However, India doesn't fall in the list of 50 Happiest Countries of the world. This is the general belief that those who work hard with honesty and sincerity are very joyful people and healthy, but with little possessions. Money can provide us more luxuries, but a joyful and healthy life can't be purchased by paying any amount of wealth as felt by Steve Jobs from his deathbed, while suffering from incurable disease. Thus a big question arises - How to lead a Joyful and healthy life and a dire need to read the present text ?

Dr. V. P. Gupta 18 October 2024

ACKNOWLEDGEMENT

This document is due to the unfailing requests of our family members to see us helping the needy persons from their childhood, which I had developed by reading the book, "Winning Friends and Influencing People" by Dale Carnegie in 1960. They wanted to share our long experiences of more than sixty years appreciating people doing good work and caring and helping peers or community members around. Almost the same was the situation of my wife Usha in early fifties and sixties during her stay in foreign countries with her parents, while her father late D.R.Goel working in the Ministry of External Affairs, who was posted in Indian embassies in different countries every three years in India. Her childhood was spent in Buenos Aires, London, Karachi, Tehran and a few more countries enroute of their ship journey helping her in inculcating many life skills since her childhood, before her marriage to me in a small town of Haryana in India.

In Usha, I found a totally different lady who is beautiful, elegant, soft spoken, truthful and always caring for others. Her soberness and kind behavior towards everyone, especially the less fortunate, passed down to our three children. Their helpful attitude towards everyone made them very likable in their schools/colleges and they are now known as friends of friends in their social circles at their place of work in India and abroad. By God's grace we're all leading a very happy family life, inculcating the same values in the next generation, which we developed into our kids in their childhood. We are very lucky to have a very religious and God fearing daughter-in-law, who developed the same values of punctuality, sincerity, loving and caring nature, and respect to elders in her both sons. We are very fortunate to have the other four grandchildren of our two daughters, who are also bringing a fair name to their parents and making us proud by their qualities of head and heart. I express my deep sense of gratitude to our three children, six grandchildren, daughter- in -law and two son-in-laws for taking care of us in our old age and for bringing a fair name to the family by their hard work, keeping in view the family values developed in them.

During my shining academic career of about 50 years, I got the opportunity in NCERT and its constituent colleges to publish a few books of chemistry, a large number of research papers and popular articles in science, chemistry, microteaching, Non- Formal Education, environmental education, creativity and other areas of my interest while working for children living in slums. After my retirement from active service, I published two books - "From Deepalpur To San Francisco" in September, 2020 and "Improving My Vocabulary" in 2023. Both these books are on Amazon and Flipkart in India, U.K., America and Australia. After publishing these books, our children asked me a few times to share our lifetime experiences of leading a very joyful and healthy life with youths and elderly persons. So this book is the result of the untiring persuasion by our children and Dr. Ajay Goel for comparing the daily routine of both of us to long living people of Japan and requesting me to share our experiences of the last 75 years with youths and persons of all ages all over the globe on how to remain healthy and happy. I am highly thankful to Dr. Ajay Goel, living in America and my family members for motivation.

Our grandchildren have been taking a very keen interest in our lifetime stories. Kunal, Yashsvi, Aryan, Krishna, Anshul and Ishana helped us a lot during our visit to them. Some of their traits are included in this text. We are thankful to them for their love, care, timely help and for learning a lot from all of them. Volley of thanks to them all. Aryan, a student of UCB and now doing his 3rd semester from the University of Barcelona, agreed to go through the manuscript very minutely. I express my special thanks to dear Aryan for sparing quite a good time from his busy schedule.

I am deeply indebted to Bobby for his very valuable suggestions after going through the manuscript very thoroughly and writing the introduction of the book. Chapter on food is added because of his suggestion only. Usha, my wife, has been a great source of inspiration to me to write this book for the benefit of the general public by following some of the attributes, as suggested by her sharp thinking while having a glance of the book at the final stage. It gives me pleasure to express my thanks to Mrs Gupta from the bottom of my heart from whom I snatched her very precious moments of her company for about a year.

Some family members, a few friends and community members of our Senior Citizens group living in our campus came forward to share their long experiences, who have been leading a very healthy and happy life at their own places in India, America, Australia and U.K. All of them deserve a big applause for suggesting very useful attributes. I can't forget the technical help rendered by my all six grandchildren as mentioned above and for sparing their laptops to me from time to time. Bobby, Shuchita, Kavita, Ramesh, Deepika, and Vineet always stood by our side with their unparalleled help while staying with them. We are lucky to have them as our children and pray to God for their good health and cheerfulness.

During the writing of this book, I had to consult Google, Wikipedia, Gemini, and AI for which I record my thanks to them all. Last but not the least, I am deeply thankful to Blue Rose publishers for bringing out this book, which may be helpful to readers in bringing cheers in their life with good health.

Dr. V.P. Gupta 18 October 2024.

INTRODUCTION

In a fast-paced world that is constantly evolving, the quest for joyful and healthy living remains a timeless pursuit. Many strive to find a balance between physical health, mental peace, and emotional well-being. Yet, the demands of modern life often pull us in different directions, making it challenging to maintain that equilibrium. This book is a heartfelt guide to navigating this journey—a roadmap to living a life that is not only healthier but also more joyful, fulfilling, and harmonious.

The essence of joyful living lies in simplicity, gratitude, and respect, while healthy living is about nurturing the mind, body, and spirit. Through a blend of timeless wisdom and modern insights, this book explores the different facets of happiness and health, encouraging readers to discover and embrace a lifestyle that brings them inner peace, contentment, and vitality. Drawing on Dr Gupta's observations, experiences, and reflections, each chapter delves into essential aspects of life, from food and fitness to relationships and passions, aiming to inspire a holistic approach to well-being.

The journey begins with the foundation of Happiness, an elusive yet essential component of a joyful life. In this chapter, the focus is on understanding what true happiness means and how to cultivate it. It encourages readers to look beyond material pursuits and find joy in the simple moments, interactions, and experiences that life offers.

Delicious & Healthy Food forms the cornerstone of physical well-being. Eating right, savoring flavors, and enjoying a balanced diet not only nourishes the body but also uplifts the spirit. This chapter highlights the importance of choosing foods that are both nutritious and enjoyable, emphasizing the role of mindful eating in leading a healthier life.

Gratitude, respect, and love are values that bind society together, fostering positive connections and a sense of belonging. In the chapters on Gratitude, Respect To All, and Love For All, the book explores how these principles can transform our interactions, reduce stress, and contribute to overall happiness. Living with gratitude allows us to appreciate what we have, respect helps in building meaningful relationships, and love, in its many forms, adds depth and warmth to our lives.

One of the key aspects of joyful and healthy living is finding purpose. The chapter on Passion For Work encourages readers to pursue their passions, whether in their professional lives or hobbies, as a means of fulfillment and personal growth. It is about finding joy in what we do, leading to a more engaged and enriched life.

Equally important is our relationship with nature and the environment. Care For Nature calls for a greater understanding of our role in preserving the natural world. Sustainable living, respecting nature, and being mindful of our ecological footprint are essential for the well-being of both the planet and ourselves.

In a society that is continually advancing, Latest Inventions & Modern Family Life examines how technology and modern conveniences have changed family dynamics, creating both opportunities and challenges. This chapter offers insights into maintaining healthy relationships amidst these changes, promoting unity and understanding within families.

The subsequent chapters further delve into the roles of Family Members, Relatives, Friends & Others, emphasizing the importance of social connections and community. Religious Places, Old Age Homes & Orphanages remind us of the value of compassion and empathy, guiding readers towards acts of kindness that bring internal happiness.

This book also celebrates the arts—Music, Dance & Paintings—as expressions of joy, creativity, and emotional release. These forms of art have the power to heal, uplift, and bring people together, enhancing the quality of life.

Lastly, no guide on joyful and healthy living would be complete without touching on self-discipline. Punctuality, Regular Exercises, Self Care & Attributes for Joyful And Healthy Living are essential practices for sustaining both mental and physical health. This chapter offers practical advice on habits and routines that can lead to a more balanced lifestyle.

Philanthropy & Some Anecdotes of Internal Happiness adds a personal touch, sharing stories that illustrate the joy of giving, while the final chapter, What We Can Do For Joyful & Healthy Living, provides actionable steps for readers to embark on their own journeys toward a fulfilling life.

Together, these chapters form a comprehensive guide that touches on every aspect of life, encouraging readers to make conscious choices for a joyful, healthy, and harmonious existence.

Enjoy the Book !

Bobby Gupta
Cofounder & CEO
Votal AI, Inc
(Ex CRO Virsec, SVP TechM , IBM)
Board Advisor and Angel Investor

TABLE OF CONTENTS

CHAPTER -1 HAPPINESS 1

CHAPTER -2 Delicious & Healthy Food 9

CHAPTER -3 GRATITUDE 20

CHAPTER – 4 RESPECT TO ALL 31

CHAPTER - 5 PASSION FOR WORK 41

CHAPTER – 6 LOVE FOR ALL, STRESSES & DEVELOPMENTS 52

CHAPTER-7 NATION FIRST REST NEXT 67

CHAPTER- 8 CARE FOR NATURE 80

CHAPTER – 9 LATEST INVENTIONS & MODERN FAMILY LIFE 94

CHAPTER-11 RELATIVES, FRIENDS & OTHERS . 116

CHAPTER-13 MUSIC, DANCE & PAINTING 153

CHAPTER – 15 PHILANTHROPY & ANECDOTES OF INTERNAL HAPPINESS 206

CHAPTER -16 WHAT WE CAN DO FOR JOYFUL AND HEALTHY LIVING 218

REFERENCES 224

CHAPTER -1
HAPPINESS

The United States of America is the richest country of the world followed by China, Germany, Japan and India as per data released by International Monetary Fund (IMF) in 2024 (1), but on the happiness index, America having population of 340 M and per capita income of US $83,061 is not the happiest country. The US is ranked as the 23rd happiest country; Germany as 24th, Japan as 47th, China as 60th and India with a population of 1440 M and per capita income of US $9183 is lagging behind. In turn, Costa Rica and Kuwait, very small countries, entered the list of top 20 at 12th and 13th place of ranking. The report submitted by Jennifer De Paola (2), a happiness researcher at the University of Helsinki on World's Happiness Day on 21st March, 2024 mentions that the happiest countries no longer included any of the world's largest or most developed countries. The happiness ranking is based on individuals' self assessed evaluations of life satisfaction, as well as GDP per capita, social support, healthy living, and healthy life expectancy. The researcher further highlights that Finland has been ranked as the happiest country of the world 7th time in a row (2). Jennifer also observes Finns' close connection to nature and healthy work- life balance as the key contributors to their life satisfaction.

The report also found that younger generations were happier than their older peers in most of the world's regions – but not all. In Australia and New Zealand, happiness among group 30 has dropped dramatically since 2006, with older generations now happier than the younger ones. Also, happiness inequality increased in every region except Europe (2).

Finland, a small European country with a population of 5.5 M and a per capita income of US $50,836 is rated as the happiest country in the world with a happiness score of 7.80. Denmark, Iceland, Sweden, Israel, The Netherlands, Norway, Luxembourg, Switzerland all very small European countries fall in line with 2nd, 3rd, 4th, 6th, 7th, 8th and 9th position and Australia with 10th ranking in the row. Surprisingly, Israel, who is currently engaged in war with Palestine, occupies 5th position, with a score of 7.34 in terms of the happiness index. Australia with GDP of US $1509 billion, population of 26.6M and per capita income of US $64693 is rated as the 10th happiest country. China with a population of about 1439 M, almost similar to India, but low per capita income of US $5451 is rated as 60th.

The above data indicates that the richest people are not supposed to be the happiest people and richest nations need not to be the happiest ones. There are many other factors that make us happy. Happiest score of different countries is based upon six categories namely GDP per capita, social support, healthy life expectancy, and freedom to make your own life choices, generosity of the general population and perception of internal and external corruption level.

Money is definitely one of the important sources of happiness, which helps us to arrange meals, transportation, and access to technology etc. Life is becoming more and more materialistic, with new inventions to make life more comfortable. Young engineers, doctors, teachers, business magnets and even youths living in huts, slums or rural areas are aware of the latest gadgets available or being launched in any part of the world, though they may not have them, but this shows a happy trend. Ready-made garments of international brands are also in reach of a person living in a remote area. Smartphones have brought the world very close to one another. There is a knowledge explosion and life is changing very fast even in the least developed areas of the world in contrast to the old notion of three basic needs namely, food, clothes and shelter (Roti, Kapda Aur Makan).

A very fast life, more facilities, more gadgets and more money are making modern man's living more comfortable but not leading to a happier life. Many of us may not be free from anxieties, worries about our own health, health of our children, parents, relatives, family members and neighbors in spite of rolling in wealth. Many questions are bound to arise in our mind. Do we have any free time to think about ourselves, elderly family members and the neighbors and talk to them? Do we ever take care of our maid / domestic help? Do we ever think of our teachers, who imparted us good education to enjoy a very comfortable life? How many of us ever find time to talk to workers of our campus, our old friends, and enquire about health issues of friends and neighbors?

Are we regular callers to our relatives, and above all do we ever enquire about the health of our parents, their daily needs while living with them or away from them? How much time do we really find daily / weekly / fortnightly / monthly / yearly to talk to parents, brothers and sisters not living with us? Do we visit parents and family members too often to spend time with them? Do we still believe in writing letters / sending emails to parents, or calling them, family members, relatives on their birthdays off and on ? Let's ponder over.

Did we ever think of helping the downtrodden people living in nearby areas and did we ever utilize our spare time to help the community of our own campus? Do we often praise our partner / children for their good conduct towards neighbors or the domestic help? Do we really praise our partner for his / her promotion? Are we in the habit of giving awards to our children for doing exemplary work in academics, sports, co-curricular and social activities in school / college and the community? Do we take our children for picnics in nearby tourist places of interest? Do we ever plan a visit with our children to some zoo / museum / science centers on weekends?

Did we ever stop on the highway after coming across some road accident? Did we ever put our life in danger to save someone in distress? Did we ever give the last coins of our wallet to feed some hungry person? How many of us dared to share our lunch with our subordinates? Did we ever ask the maid servant for a glass of water or asked for a cup of tea and snacks after finishing cleanliness work of our house? Did we ever praise our competitor at our learning place for doing exceptionally well or on his / her promotion? Some of us must be following these attributes. If not, we can try and feel the intense waves of happiness penetrating in our body just after our positive action.

Did our parents take our opinion about the career we are involved in and are we enjoying our present job? Are we working honestly and diligently in office and are we loyal to our company? Are we contributing for the betterment of the society / community where we reside? Do we think that our job helps for the progress of the Nation? Are we democratic in our approach while arguing with our colleagues? Are we a good listener or an excellent orator? Do we give patient listening to our husband / wife or children? Do we listen to our boss with rapt attention? Do we ever think of giving suggestions for the betterment of the company where we are working? How many times did we quarrel with our neighbors while parking our vehicles? Did we ever invite our neighbors for a cup of tea / coffee? Are we punctual in every walk of life? Do we ever feel sometimes that we become inconvenient to our colleagues due to our punctuality, sincerity to work and working with honesty at the workplace? Do we ever say hello even to strangers with a smile during morning / evening walk? Are we in the habit of getting up early in the morning? Do we still believe in the proverb "Early to bed and early to rise, makes a man healthy, wealthy and wise"?

Have we ever offered a seat while traveling in a bus for an elderly person or some ailing boy /girl? Do we give a phone call to friends / relatives on their birthday /

anniversary or prefer to send a message to save time? Do we subscribe to a newspaper or prefer to get news from our mobile? Do we prefer to engage our baby with a mobile to get busy without crying or do we like to have interesting conversations with our children and family members in our free time? Do we cut jokes with friends and go for leisurely walks? Do we like singing or listening to old songs? Can we guess when we had a big laugh in the company of friends or family members? Do we like hosting parties for friends / neighbors or relatives at home or prefer to enjoy parties at friends' houses / restaurants? Do we visit our birth place and meet family members/ elderly people / relatives sometimes in spite of our busy schedule? Do we take small gifts for family members during visits or avoid thinking that they don't need anything? Do we like to have pets at home? While taking the pet outside for natural needs, do we take a carry bag? Do we keep our pet in chains while going for a walk? Have we got our pet vaccinated? Do we take the pet to the veterinary doctor for a regular check up?

We can respond to the above questions by taking our own time. Answers may be in yes, or no. We are the judge of ourselves and can make an honest opinion about ourselves after going through our responses. Some of us may be very happy after reading responses and some may think otherwise. Some of us may think of changing our behavior at home, office, in the company of friends, family members and relatives. We may become a good father, good mother, good husband or a good wife, become a loyal friend and may become a very useful citizen of the society or the community where we are living. We can become good bosses, good employees, good neighbors, and above all become good human beings leading us to a very healthy and happy life.

By performing the above simple activities in our day to day life, we get internal happiness due to the release of certain chemicals and Hormones like dopamine, endorphins, serotonin and oxytocin in our brain. We feel happy if we perform a few activities given below in our daily life and analyze the change in our body:

1. Feeding a cow or dog in the morning by our own hands.
2. Talking to cleaner cleaning roads of our campus and enquiring about his / her health.
3. Offering a cup of tea to binbag young boy / girl around our campus.
4. Sharing our tiffin with our class fellows / office workers.
5. Offering a seat in the bus to a standing peer or old person

After performing these acts, write your feelings in our diary and share with your parents or colleagues and observe their reaction.

Let's remain happy and healthy by following some of the above mentioned traits and also try to make an atmosphere of happiness around us, so that everyone is found to be happy on this planet. We are the children of God, by whose grace only, our parents happened to bring us on this planet. Expressing our sincere gratitude and thanks to

The Almighty, our parents and elderly persons and exhibiting our love to youths and children of our campus can definitely make us a happier person.

CHAPTER -2
DELICIOUS & HEALTHY FOOD

Food is an important part for sustainable life. Mother's milk is said to be the best food for the newborn baby for the first six months. After that the child starts getting very soft diets consisting of soup of pulses, porridge or cracked wheat grains after boiling with milk and some component of sugar followed by well cooked light pulses and rice with small amounts of cow ghee (molten butter) and sugar. Mother milk, cow milk, pulses, porridge and rice are said to be the complete diet for a child to fulfill requirements of necessary proteins, vitamins and carbohydrates. With growth of the child there is a requirement of better supplements of proteins, vitamins, oils, fats and carbohydrates. Mothers take care of school going children to serve them with a balanced diet but delicious to enjoy. As children grow, they develop taste for different edibles available in their areas, without taking care of their food value.

India is a country of unity in diversity with different seasons in different parts of vast India. similar is the case with other countries with different climatic conditions. In northern India wheat, maize, rice, Sugarcane, mustard and chickpea (Chana) are the main crops making north Indians to consume breads of wheat and maize in different seasons along with different kinds of leafy vegetables. Potatoes, onions, tomatoes, carrots, radish, cabbage, cauliflowers, bottle gourd, bitter bottle gourd, pumpkin, ridge gourd and sponge gourd are very popular vegetables. Though pumpkin, bottle gourd, Ridge gourd, capsicum, cabbage, cauliflower and bitter bottle gourd are very light and healthy vegetables but rarely liked by northern Indian youths. They are liked only by elderly people or persons having some ailments. Potato is said to be the king of vegetables as it can be mixed with various types of other vegetables like cabbage, cauliflower, brinjal (egg plant), capsicum and leafy vegetables like spinach, fenugreek etc. Potatoes, tomatoes, onions and garlic are highly consumed vegetables in India. All our family members like potatoes stuffed paratha with a lot of home made butter or Amul butter produced in Amul dairy of Anand in Gujarat and buttermilk. It's my weakness too but now we have minimized its use in our family due to health problems. Potato Paratha with butter and curd followed by sweet porridge is a welcome breakfast for special guests in the morning. Butter chicken with naan and biryani are favorites non-vegetarian foods of the North. Garlic naan and tandoori breads are quite favorites of both vegetarians and non- vegetarians.

Potatoes and sweet potatoes contain a lot of starch, overuse of which may lead to development of diabetes. North Indians are also very fond of sweets, which is again the main source of obesity and diabetes. Use of beer is also very common, but it's overuse also leads to obesity and damage to the liver. Smoking is another bad habit in growing children of adolescent age, due to which youths become addicted to smoking and drinking. This is due to these bad habits that youths of Haryana and

Punjab have become drug addicts spoiling their names, which were earlier known as states of wrestlers, boxers, shooters and athletes of world fame winning medals in Olympics. These don't constitute healthy diets and need to be avoided from the early stage.

The states of Haryana, Punjab, Uttar Pradesh, and Rajasthan are known for the best quality of cows and buffaloes. They are the maximum milk producing states along with Gujarat. Amul Dairy milk is popular throughout northern India and now it has started exporting to a few neighboring countries. Mothers Dairy of Delhi is also fulfilling needs of Delhiites besides the needs of a few adjoining states. Milk, butter, curd, cheese, ice cream and ghee of Amul Dairy, Mother Dairy and milk dairies of adjoining states of Rajasthan, Uttar Pradesh, Himachal Pradesh and Uttarakhand are doing yeoman service in northern India. This could be possible only due to white revolution known as the world's biggest dairy development program, led by Dr. Verghese Kurien started in 1970. This white revolution transformed a dairy- deficient nation into the global leader in milk production, and we are proud of our achievements responsible for the good health of north Indians.

Milk and milk products like curd, buttermilk, cheese, butter, ghee and other dairy products and sweets made from milk / milk products are full of proteins, vitamins, fats, many minerals and lactose carbohydrates. Lactose is a disaccharide sugar of molecular formula $C_{12}H_{22}O_{11}$. Lactose is transformed by lactase, an enzyme into glucose

and fructose which are simpler sugars falling in the category of monosaccharides with molecular formula C6H12O6. Both these monosaccharide sugars are used by our body for energy and various other functions. Some people have difficulty in digesting lactose due to their body structure.

Japanese are found to be the healthiest persons with the highest longevity in the world. Generally they never eat while walking, they never take soup or tea with food instead of cold drinks, they never overeat and they also take probiotic substances like curd or yogurt, cheese, coconut, sour cream, cottage cheese etc. For our good health we may include a few of the probiotic substances in our food. Probiotic foods contain beneficial bacteria that can provide a large number of benefits (Generative AI, 24 Feb. 2023) as given below:

1. **Improved Digestion** - Probiotics help in improving digestion and in relieving constipation.

2. **Stronger Immune System** - They help in strengthening the immune system by preventing the growth of harmful bacteria and promoting a healthy inflammation response.

3. **Reduce Risk of Infection** - Probiotics may help prevent and treat infectious diarrhea caused by viruses and bacteria.

4. **Less Risk of Chronic Disease** - Probiotics help in reducing inflammation and protect from chronic diseases.

5. **Improved Metabolism** - They help in improving metabolism
6. **Improved Mental Health** - Probiotics also help in improving mental health.
7. **Reduces Risk of Cancer** - Probiotics help in reducing the levels of carcinogenic substances in the gut.
8. **Improved Lactose Intolerance** - They also help in improving lactose intolerance.

Newborn babies live only on mother's milk for the first six months. Milk is said to be the complete diet and many Indian sages live only on cow milk. One glass of buttermilk with breakfast, one bowl of curd during lunch and one glass of milk without sugar before sleeping leads to better health and happiness due to the presence of probiotic enzymes in them.

Other popular couisines and snacks of northern India are chhole Bhature, Chhole Kulche, Samosa and stuffed Kachori. Rajasthani kachori with hot curry is very fondly eaten by residents of Rajasthan, but it's too hot to digest. Even then people enjoy this preparation. Rajasthan is also popular for Yellow dal and Baatis (made from coarse flour of wheat and chickpea). A few parts of the state of Rajasthan was desert, where no greenery was visible for miles and miles together with sand dunes. Camels were the only source of transport and the travelers used to go for trading only by riding the camels. There were bushes here and there. travelers used to carry wheat and chickpea flour and yellow lentil with them and used to prepare dal and batis by burning dried branches of bushes. But Dal and Bati with butter has also become a very popular cuisine in marriages taking place in Rajasthan, Madhya Pradesh and in many states of India and even in some foreign countries..

Chhole Bhature, Dal Bati, Samosas and Kachoris are very oily, which don't fall in the category of healthy food items. They can be used off and on, but their continuous use is detrimental for health. Malwa region of Madhya Pradesh has a very good reputation for very light and healthy Poha as a part of snacks. Dal and rice with bottled gourd or ridge gourd vegetables are very healthy food items, which are very useful for everyone, especially the elderly people. Such light vegetables and snacks used with curd are quite good for our health.

South India is known for very healthy food items like fermented rice with curd, and lentil dishes like Dosa, Idli and Sambar. Idli is prepared from Rice flour or semolina (coarse wheat flour) mixed with curd and steamed in an Idli cooker. This edible item is free from oil and fat and is used as such with sambar made from lentils. Idli sambhar is a very healthy and popular south Indian cuisine but is now available throughout India and other southern countries breaking all barriers. This dish can be made within half an hour and ready for serving to unannounced guests. Sambar and Dosa is another very popular south Indian dish served with stuffed potatoes, onions and tomatoes or without any vegetable, easily digestible and extremely good for health. Coconuts are widely grown on the seashores of south India. People of south India use coconut in almost every preparation and coconut oil is the major oil of South Indians. Coconut oil is very healthy for hair i.e. why ladies of south India have dark black long hair. More use of spices like cloves, black peppers and turmeric and lots of vegetables in sambar and the least use of oil make south Indians healthier people. As rice is easily digested and south Indians don't use much butter or ghee, they generally have thin structures as compared to north Indians who consume a lot of oil, fat and sweets besides regular consumption of milk. Most of the South Indians are generally considered quite intelligent people in India.

We are quite fond of south Indian dishes at home in India or abroad. Usha, Shuchita, Kavita, and Deepika are experts in making very delicious south Indian dishes though we are not south Indians. We and all family members relish south Indian dishes as well besides northern dishes. I recall with great fondness and appreciation the pizza party held at Bobby's house, where various kinds of pizzas were prepared unstopped for 20 guests by Aryan. Aryan kept standing by his pizza oven and prepared pizzas for three hours. Aryan was showered with blessings by all guests for his unparalleled loving act for the guests by proving his family values inculcated in him from very childhood. Aryan got extreme happiness by serving food to guests and made us all content by relishing pizzas with lots of inner happiness to one and all..

During our Europe trip with Kunal, we couldn't find any Indian restaurant open at 10 pm in the night, but Kunal navigated us to an Italian restaurant, where we got pizza and a bottle of coke. We three had a good fill after enjoying the new dish in Paris. Pasta is another dish made of semolina, which we have started enjoying even in Indian cities. Domino's and KFC have opened their chains in many cities of India and many other countries. Youths have become very fond of pizza, pasta and vegetarian and non-vegetarian burgers. We also do enjoy these Italian and American dishes once in a while for a change and at our son's place in America and at our daughters' places at Indore and Australia. As samosa, kachori and chhole bhature have crossed boundaries of India and are easily available in different cities and many developed countries, Italian pizza, pasta and american fast food have become very popular delicacies in India and many other Asian countries.

Being a vegetarian, I am not much acquainted with non - veg dishes, but heard a lot about butter chicken with naan as the most favorite of Indians and foreigners. People living on the seashores develop a habit of enjoying seafoods like fishes, prawns and dishes made from other aquatic animals. Fish is rich in calcium and phosphorus and a great source of minerals, such as iron, zinc, iodine, magnesium and potassium. Fish is filled with omega -3 fatty acids and vitamins such as D and B2 also known as riboflavin. Fish oil is highly useful for good health in many ways (Generative AI) as given below:

1. **Heart Health** -Fish oil may reduce triglycerides, lower blood pressure, and raise HDL (good) cholesterol, which may lower heart disease, stroke, and blood clots. However, there are some contradicting views as well.

2. **Blood Pressure** - Some studies suggest that fish oil supplements may reduce blood pressure, especially in people with moderate to severe high blood pressure.

3. **Rheumatoid Arthritis** - Fish oil supplements may help reduce pain, stiffness, and joint tenderness in people with rheumatoid arthritis..

4. **Eye Health** - Fish oil may lower triglyceride levels and reduce the risk of heart attack or developing age-related macular degeneration (AMD).

5. **Brain Health** - Fish oil may help with attention, immediate recall, and processing speed.

6. **Ulcers** - Animal studies suggest that cod liver oil may help treat stomach and gut ulcers. Keeping so many uses of fish oil in view, it is also added to many foods, including milk, yogurt, cereal, chocolate, cookies, and juices of many fruits for better health of people of old age.

A good meal can stimulate the release of the feel-good hormone, dopamine. A study in humans suggests that dopamine release in the brain occurs at two different times - at the time the food is first ingested and another once the food reaches the stomach. Endorphins are other happiness hormones that are associated with feeling enchantment.

The following suggestions may be useful for readers to make use of exercises and healthy food for better health:

1. Day to be started with one glass of hot water in sitting posture and sipping water slowly.

2. Persons suffering from diabetes may dip one spoon of fenugreek grains in one glass of water in the night, drink its water in the next morning and then chew grains slowly. This practice may be avoided in summers when temperature is more than 35 degree celsius

3. Diabetic persons should take a cup of tea without sugar.

4. 30 minutes of Yoga and 15 minutes of stretching exercises daily keep us healthy.

5. A 30 minute morning walk and a 30 minute evening walk in some garden or open space helps keep us fit throughout the day.

6. Light breakfast of poha, Idli sambar, porridge, cereal with milk or two pieces of bread with butter and milk may keep you fit till lunch time. Breakfast can be replaced by fruits or two glasses of buttermilk. Never start your day without breakfast.

7. Lunch may be taken between 1.00 - 2.00 pm depending upon office work. Easily digested light vegetables to form part of a tiffin with one dal and one bowl of curd with a pinch of salt and black pepper. Lunch can also be replaced by raw fruits including an apple. Meals never

to be taken in haste. Small leaves of bread with chewing 32 times is said to be very useful for digestion of meals.

8. Evening tea without sugar with some snacks.
9. Dinner to be taken at least 2 hours before going to bed.
10. One glass of hot milk, better with one spoon of turmeric.

CHAPTER -3
GRATITUDE

Gratitude and happiness are very closely interlinked. Expressing thankfulness to God may be a powerful tool to cultivate happiness and contentment in our life. We may or may not believe in God but we must accept that there is some superpower controlling the universe and that superpower is considered God by people of different nationalities following different religions in different ways. In Hindu mythology, besides worshiping any God of one's own choice, some of us treat even Water, Air, Fire, Earth, and Sun as subgods as they fulfill our daily needs. So we worship them. Pure air is most essential for life. A normal person has to breathe oxygen from air 10-15 times in one minute. But industrial development clubbed with more and more multi storey buildings and development of infrastructures in cosmopolitan cities and big towns are polluting air leading to many ailments in children and adults. Asthmatic problems are very common in children and elderly persons over there. Pure water is another essential component of life. Citizens of many countries are facing scarcity of drinking water. If potable water resources are decreasing day by day, they are constantly polluted by various effluents coming from industries and humans' waste entering lakes and rivers, which are the sources of drinking water. Lakes and rivers are drying making life more stressful for living beings - humans, animals, birds and agriculturists around the globe. How many of us ever think to save water, air, atmosphere and above all our earth to keep all living beings healthy and happy. We can make concerted efforts to minimize air and water pollution by planting more and more trees around our residential areas and also by conserving and harvesting water.

Sun is the most powerful source of natural energy, which helps to keep us and our earth warm. Crops, plants, and all types of fauna and flora grow only by sun energy besides water and manure or fertilizers. Life on earth would not have been possible without the Sun. In India and many other countries, most people worship the rising Sun daily by offering water in the morning to express their gratitude for their survival on this planet. Basking in sunlight or morning walk for 10-15 minutes from 8.00 to 9.00 am is very beneficial as sunlight rays during this period provide us vitamin D (3) to make up for vitamin deficiency and we remain healthy. Generally speaking, Vitamin D is also called "the sunshine vitamin", the reason being that when our skin is exposed to sunlight, it makes vitamin D from cholesterol. The sun's ultraviolet B (UVB) rays hit cholesterol in the skin cells, providing energy for vitamin D synthesis in our body.

Green plants and certain organisms present on earth transform light energy from the Sun into chemical energy by the phenomenon of photosynthesis (4,5,6). During photosynthesis in green plants, light energy is captured by chlorophyll and used to convert water, carbon dioxide, and minerals into oxygen and energy - rich glucose. The process seems to be very complex, but can be summarized with the help of chemical equation given below :

$6CO_2 + 6H_2O = C_6H_{12}O_6 + 6O_2$ (in the presence of Chlorophyll and sunlight)

The following events occur during the process of photosynthesis :

(a). Absorption of light energy by chlorophyll,

(b). Conversion of light energy to chemical energy and splitting of water molecules into hydrogen and oxygen,

(c). Reduction of carbon dioxide to carbohydrates.

Solar energy is being adopted by developed and developing countries like India as the substitute of thermal energy to control air pollution and global warming to save the Earth. If the majority of countries start following Solar, wind or tidal energy as alternatives to thermal energy, this will be our greatest gratitude to mother earth and we can lead a joyful and healthy life.

Different religions treat different super souls as their God and worship them accordingly to bless them, their family members, their community, their cattle, their land, plants, trees, forests, rivers, seas and all living beings with longevity, prosperity and cheerfulness. Hindus construct temples in the name of God, Muslims construct mosques for prayers, Sikhs and Christians have Gurdwaras and Churches as places of worship respectively. There are many more religions and their followers adopt different ways of prayers to The Almighty to express their gratitude.

We may start the day by expressing gratitude to our God by sitting in silence for a few minutes. Some of us may be visiting the place of worship after finishing morning chores in the nearby area. There are many people who devote a very long time to prayers by using a Microphone system. Some devotees worship to show off their love for God. While praying to God, we should try to be with Him with full concentration, maybe for one minute, but away from all domestic or official worries. God is our well wisher and nothing is hidden from Him. God is present everywhere and omnipotent and takes care of us all. A true follower of God always remains happy and cheerful as he considers God always within him / her and other living beings. Such a person always treats all human beings as the subjects of the same Almighty, as God is present in everyone of us on this planet. Even plants, animals, birds are blessed by God. Our rivers, streams, and oceans are blessed by God. If there are thousands of living species on land, there are large numbers of aquatic animals in rivers and oceans. By taking care of living beings around us, we are making our God happy.

We may come across highly religious people performing varieties of religious rituals but not treating subjects of God with love and care. We may find a very large number of hypocrites in our own neighborhood / locality, who pretend to be highly religious in the community but in their daily dealings, they are not kind hearted towards poor persons or homeless wanderers. Some of the rich people take undue advantage of the poverty of needy people to achieve their hidden agenda. About three hundred years ago, developed western countries used to take people from underdeveloped countries of Asia and Africa for farming in their fields and working as slaves at their homes. Slavery was very common in those days. Indians settled in Fiji islands, Mauritius and a few other countries were shipped from U.P. and Bihar as slaves for growing sugarcane. They were never treated as human beings. They were subjected to various kinds of torture. They were rarely given sufficient food to satisfy their daily hunger and never a respectable place to live in and never providing daily use items for their well- being.

When Europeans first colonized the North American continent, they found vast land, but there was a severe shortage of labor. Being in search of labor, a Dutch ship loaded with African slaves solved the problem of cheap labor in the early seventeenth century. This was the beginning of slavery system (7) in America and many other rich countries. Such slaves proved economical for growing cash crops of tobacco, sugarcane and rice, as they were provided only a very few basic minimums just to survive. The landlords became very wealthy, holding high positions in the society but by exploiting the basic rights of workers. Asian countries also did not remain untouched. Big landlords started exploiting poor people not having any land for cultivation or even for constructing their own house to live in. Such landless people were kept as their bonded labors for helping their families in daily chores, cultivating their lands and for looking after their cattle. Most of the Lords used to follow their religion, worshiping God of their faith but they cared the least for their bonded laborers/ slaves. They never worshiped God with pure heart due to their selfish motives. Such cruel people, not thankful to God, have to pay the price one day due to their misdeeds towards poor persons working for them at homes or their offices. Such people not caring for poor ones can never be happy.

The slavery system continued in America till 1865 after the 13th Amendment to the U.S. constitution even after getting independence on July 4, 1776. Martin Luther King Jr. (8), an American Christian minister, kept raising his voice for civil rights of such persons from 1955 until 1968, when he was assassinated. There is no dearth of people exploiting the poor men and women in many parts of the world to satisfy their lust for power, snatching more land from poor countries and more wealth, but they can never be happy. They are restless, egoistic, obstinate fellows and can't have a sound sleep like normal God - fearing poor people, who always keep them busy with their work.

Russia - Ukraine war has been going on for the last more than two years, killing thousands of civilians- most of them ladies, expectant mothers and innocent children. What's their fault? They are not participating in the war, so why are they being made the target? Are they not the children of God? God loves them a lot. God resides within them as well, but even then they are made to suffer. Such war criminals don't believe in God or they are thankless towards God. They can't have a good sleep, due to anxieties of their crimes and will never lead a happy and peaceful life.

More heinous crimes are being committed by Israeli forces also. They have killed more than 40,000 innocent people since 7th October, 2023 after the Hamas attack. Most of the Airmen, and Army men fighting for Israel / America are Christians and believe in Christianity, worship by going to church, but they follow orders of their commanders to kill innocent civilians. Some of the right thinking army have started realizing the crime being committed. Very recently, a 25 year - old airman, Aaron Bushnell (9) of the US air force has died after he set himself ablaze outside the Israeli embassy in Washington D. C., while declaring that he "will no longer be complicit in genocide". The incident occurred on Feb. 25, 2024 as Israeli Prime Minister; Benjamin Netanyahu was seeking cabinet approval for a military operation in the southern Gaza city while a temporary ceasefire deal was being negotiated. The Israeli Government didn't show any interest to abide by the ceasefire resolution passed by UNO for stopping the war and started talking with Palestine / Hamas authorities for finding some amicable solution. The Israeli government didn't care for listening to the American authorities, who were supporting them earlier for defeating Hamas.

Another heart touching story is of killing hundreds of Palestinian children, who were collecting ration for running their families. Main task for the forces is always to defeat the enemy forces while taking care of the civilians. Had they been true followers of their religion / God, and really thankful to God for whatever they were having, they shouldn't have attacked the innocent people and encroached upon their land. Almost similar type of genocide has been taking place on civilians of a very small country of Ukraine by Russia, a super power for encroachment of their land for more than two years since Feb. 2022. In spite of being a very small country with limited resources and limited number of weapons, fighter planes, tanks and armory in comparison to the mighty Russia, Ukrainian forces and people are giving a commendable fight to Russian forces. In Russia also there are many right thinking civilians and military personnel, but the opinion of such members is rarely making any impact on the egoistic and stubborn authorities of Russia. Russian opposition politician Alexei Navalny was close to being freed in a prisoner swap at the time of his death, but President Putin could not tolerate the thought of his release. Alexei Navalny, Russian opposition leader (10) 47, died at an Arctic penal colony on Feb.16, 2024. Such invaders can never be happy and can never lead a joyful life by carrying out such genocide on a large scale. Our leader, Mahatma Gandhi preached for non-violence throughout his freedom struggle of India from South Africa, but he also became a victim of violence on Jan. 30 1948. Such heads of states or individuals may be successful in achieving their immediate goals by following tactics of force, violence and genocide on a very large scale, but they can never be happy.

Happy are those persons who always believe to have God with them at every moment, taking care of needy persons, feeding hungry, extending a helping hand towards poor people and engaged in social work for the community. Such persons always enjoy a joyful life and always remain happy by making others happy by their inner thoughts and deeds. They also get blessings from The Almighty. Many Hindus and Indians of other religions too worship many trees like Neem (Azadirachta indica), Peepal (Ficus religiosa), Bargad (Ficus benghalensis), Tulsi, Holi Basil (Ocimum tenuiflorum) and many more, as they have medicinal values. It's a part of their daily routine in most of the families that before starting the day, they convey their thanks to God. Tulsi plant is worshiped after taking a shower and offering water and lighting a lamp every morning and evening. Bark, leaves and fruits of Neem trees have antiseptic values. Gel and juice of Aloe Vera plant are widely used for skin shine, healing the wounds, for asthmatic and diabetic patients. Millions of people all over the globe are enjoying good health by worshiping, and taking care of medicinal plants and they remain happy. By planting such useful trees, people express their thankfulness to God / nature. Many people throughout the world worship plants and trees as gifts of God to give them food, shelter and protect them from various diseases and various kinds of calamities. Watering the plants in our kitchen garden and taking care of them by proper manure and sunlight is a good exercise for remaining healthy for elderly as well as young people. Trimming plants from time to time helps them to grow and to add beauty to our kitchen garden besides enhancing our happiness and good health. The old proverb "Health is Wealth" should be the thought for everyday for everyone and for us all.

Americans are very God fearing people. They are very affluent with highest GDP and per capita income by having big industries, highly rated universities with excellent infrastructure, highly qualified scientific, technical, linguistic, humanity and other subjects' faculty members with highest number of patents to their credit, largest number of Nobel laureates, and above all the strongest Military Power of the world. But they have a great system of Thanksgiving to God, parents, teachers, friends and their neighbors. This is a very good custom of Americans when most of them visit their parents, friends and others on the last Thursday of November for Thanksgiving by staying with them, sharing their feelings and listening to the parents followed by lunch / dinner with them during the last weekend. Such a family get together taking place quite often in a year acts as a health booster and brings positivity and happiness to all members of the family. Sharing of problems and anxieties faced by most of us in our hectic life with family members and friends act as a panacea, which is most important to lead a joyful and healthy life. There is a long weekend throughout the country for such an ideal Thanksgiving ceremony. Such a custom to convey our thanks to God / parents/ teachers / friends / neighbors and even to our children may be followed by citizens of other countries to keep us all happy and healthy.

Asian countries were known for their joint family system until a few years ago. Every couple used to have 5-6 children in Joint families. Bringing up children was not a problem for parents as there used to be many members to look after the newly born kids. This used to keep all members very busy, happy and healthy as each family also had 3-4 cattle, which were a source of pure milk, curd, cheese and other milk products. Joint family system is fading away these days as a result of which the newly wedded couples find it very difficult even to bring up one or two kids. But in India, some pockets have still been following a joint family system and it is very difficult to believe that as many as 50-60, 100- 120, 200-250 family members of 3-4 generations live together in different pockets of India and in other countries. There was an unbelievable news item from Indore (INDIA) very recently to highlight the importance of the joint family system when one joint family had 345 members living together and all enjoying their food under one kitchen. All family members enjoy good health and very rarely take some medicine.

Let's try to remain healthy and enjoy a joyful life by making others happy and always conveying our thanks / gratitude to God/ parents / teachers and all around us.

1. Let's offer a small packet of biscuits to the security guard of your campus while returning from office and see a change of happiness in your mind and Body.
2. Let's share our tiffin with others.
3. Even one sentence of appreciation to a worker on our campus can make him /her very happy. Let's try while returning home.

CHAPTER – 4
RESPECT TO ALL

Since the beginning of life on earth, when humans were living in forests, might was right. But with the passage of time, came the concept of family/tribe. People living in families or tribes set some rules to lead a peaceful life. Various civilizations came into existence in different continents around water bodies as water was the immediate need for life besides food and fire. Every family, community, society is run by a few sets of traditions. In Indian culture, on any important activity like birth of a child, first day in school, in college, first day of getting a job, tying a knot with a life partner, celebrating birthday or marriage anniversary, parents / grandparents and other elderly family members are given respect by having their feet touched, who in turn bless their children. Parents, grandparents and teachers keep wishing good luck and prosperity to children, grandchildren and their students every moment. Such gestures or others are quite common all over the world on special occasions. If we Indians and Asians take blessings by worshiping our Gods and touching the feet of our elders, people living in other countries have their own ways of blessing their children or friends by hugging and kissing.

Expressing respect and regards to elders and others makes us cheerful and successful in our ventures by wishes coming from the core of the heart of the person sitting or standing before us. This is a general belief that if someone is humble and respectful to others, happiness and success is bound to come to you. We do better work, when we are cheerful as we involve our mind with full concentration without any worry, tension or ill will towards anyone. Paying respect to others makes us more humble. Even if our competitor or our enemy expresses words of appreciation to us, shows respect to us, listens to us with rapt attention, giving us positive feedback with purity of heart, we will reciprocate the same doubly and there will be an ambience of happiness around us and our competitor leading to better health to both of us or our coworkers.

Respect to others comes from within our way of living, our dealings with peers, seniors, juniors, community members, office or campus workers, domestic helpers, maids, paupers and even unknown people. Ill and unwanted behavior towards domestic help has become quite common these days. Strangely enough, stories come from very well to do families and people holding very high positions about torturing their domestic help. How many educated people and officers holding very prestigious positions can be so cruel to maids? Domestic help is rarely available and very costly in western countries. When we go abroad to meet our children, we find that they have to do all the domestic work themselves and they do very happily due to the lack of availability of maids / domestic help. But some wealthy persons take maids with them for performing daily chores for them or engage regular maids available in that country on a regular basis. Most of the wealthy people are very kind hearted and take full care of their domestic help. They make them regular payments, but there are often some cases of ill behavior. Some of the wealthy people of developed nations start torturing maids / domestic help by not providing them proper food, clothes and other facilities as per norms of that country, which is not permissible as per law of the land.

Skilled persons from many Asian countries migrate to the developed countries in search of better jobs to earn more money leaving behind their families at home. There are many incidents of ill behavior and torture on the migratory population. Passports of the migrating skilled labor are deposed by companies, so that they may not return to their land even in case of emergency and exigency at their homes. Such behavior on their part is unwanted and spoils the national image. They may be very wealthy or high officials, but can never have peace of mind and sound sleep due to their misdeeds towards people working for them. Honesty, ethical work culture, purity of heart and respect to all makes everyone happy. The following story of "A priest and a thief" may be helpful to understand the importance of purity of heart, respect for friend, sincerity to work and honesty in our daily life:

Some pooja (worship) was going on in a family in a village with the priest describing the story of Lord Krishna. House owner and most of the villagers present over there were engrossed in listening to the story of Krishna taking cows of the village outside for grazing. In the meantime, one thief entered the house to steal valuable ornaments and some coins. He searched the whole house but couldn't find anything. The thief also joined the audience and started listening to the story. The priest mentioned that Krishna's mother Yashoda being very rich used to decorate the body of Krishna from top to bottom daily with various types of gold ornaments and diamonds present in the house before sending her son with cows for grazing.

Pooja was over and the priest came out of the house. The thief, not finding valuables in the house, followed the priest and asked about the address of Krishna, as Krishna was now the only source of his income. The priest was bewildered and asked him, "Who are you"? The thief very honestly said "I am a thief, came to the house to steal valuables, but couldn't find anything of my use. Now I want to take all the ornaments from Krishna's body". The priest to get rid of the foolish thief asked him to go to the forest and he will find Krishna coming with cows in the evening after grazing them. The thief started walking towards the forest and he climbed a tree to have a close look of Krishna coming with his cows from a distance. He kept waiting, but Krishna was not visible. He got down and again climbed the tree the next day after eating some fruits from the forest. He waited and waited but Krishna didn't come. Seven days passed, but he didn't lose hope because he had great respect and faith for the priest. On the 8th day, when he was waiting for Krishna from the top branch of the tree in the evening, he saw some light penetrating towards him through the dust of the forest and saw a boy coming towards the tree. The thief became very happy, got down from the tree and started waiting for Krishna to snatch his ornaments. After some time, the thief saw a boy studded with ornaments of gold, diamond, ruby etc.

The handsome boy was emitting light. Scores of cows were following Krishna. The thief asked Krishna to stop. Krishna asked him "Who are you"? The thief said, "I am a thief. I have been waiting for you for the last eight days. You came very late. I will kill you and take all your ornaments". Krishna was very happy to listen to his plain speaking. Krishna asked him not to kill him but spread his cloth sheet hanging on his shoulders. I will take out all ornaments and you can take them. The thief was very glad to have so many glittering ornaments on his sheet, but all of a sudden the picture of the priest flashed before his mind. He didn't touch the ornaments. He decided to give half of them to the priest first as he was the person who advised him. The thief started walking towards the village with a pile of ornaments in his sheet and resolved to share half of them with the priest.

The Thief was getting restless. He started running towards the house of the priest. After reaching the priest's house, the thief narrated the whole story and asked him to have half of the ornaments as he was the instrument to find Krishna with glittering ornaments. The priest couldn't believe that the thief could meet Krishna, which he couldn't even after giving sermons to villagers during his worship of Lord Krishna for so many years. The priest insisted on taking him to see Krishna. The priest and the thief decided to go to the forest the next morning. They reached the same tree, climbed on that and kept waiting for Krishna. The same light appeared in the evening. The thief asked the priest to see the light coming towards them. But the priest couldn't see any light. The thief and the priest got down from the tree to meet Krishna. Thief was extremely happy to see the same handsome boy again with golden ornaments, but the priest couldn't see Krishna. Then the priest asked the thief that he was unable to see Lord Krishna. On the priest's desperation Krishna said to the priest "You have always been busy in narrating my story to the villagers by taking offerings but never concentrating on me very sincerely. This thief is very honest, waited for me for eight days in the forest living only on fruits to meet me and very honestly told me to snatch my ornaments as he was a thief. Krishna asked the priest to take half of my ornaments, but you can't see me. Lord Krishna asked the thief and the priest to go to their village but taking a promise of not stealing anything in future as he is a wealthy person now". Lord also advised the priest to concentrate on Krishna consciousness while giving sermons to the public". This story was narrated to me by my elder sister-in-law, Mrs Nirmla Gupta (10A) on March 1, 2024.

After reading this story, we may appreciate the thief for his honesty, truthfulness, sincerity, respect and faith for the priest. These are the core values, which always help us to be joyful and to make us healthy bodily and spiritually.

We may not be misled by the notion that only parents, elderly persons in the family or the community and teachers or company bosses need to be respected. Equally important is the duty of parents, elderly persons, teachers or the boss to respect young children, students, and the employees. The old English proverb "spare the rod and spoil the child" doesn't carry any meaning these days. This can be elaborated by the following episodes:

If a university professor tries to engage their class only by delivering the lecture full of facts and figures continuously for an hour, without paying any attention to students, there will be boredom in the class without much learning to some of the students. On the other hand, if another professor after clarifying a concept, asks a question in the class to test understanding of the concept, and uses some positive reinforcement to appreciate correct responses of students; this will definitely increase further participation of students and turn the class into a joyful place of learning. The second professor has motivated students to respond and remain active. A successful teacher never loses temper in class even after getting an incorrect response or no response. In such a case the teacher may rephrase the question and may ask another question related to the same concept. The job of a good teacher is to generate thinking in students by motivating them and creating challenging situations for better learning. This act of the teacher creates an atmosphere of happiness in the classroom with increased participation of more students. Similarly, employees also deserve the same respect from the boss as the boss expects from employees. This is a two-way traffic and the company where the employer respects employees, takes care of their needs, employees will be doubly happy to work wholeheartedly for the company to reach new heights. Many employers treat their employees as their family members. Such companies always earn more profit and there will be an ambience of cheerfulness throughout the year.

Everyone bigger or smaller needs respect. Even children in the family expect love and polite behavior from their parents and grandparents.

Fighting among over trivial issues is becoming very common. This can be minimized if they develop the habit of mutual respect and regard among their day to day activities. A true friend is someone who cares for his or her friend more than themselves. Friends have to give space to each other. Some of us are in the habit of talking and talking, without listening to other members of the group. This happens in offices, friend circles and even in families. Everyone needs some space to express his /her views for better solution of a problem, if any. We should listen to them with patience and care.

No one is perfect. There is a common saying, "To Err is Human, but to forgive is Divine." We are to ignore the mistakes or some unwanted habits of our friends, relatives or family members. In such a situation, someone is to act as a counselor. Friendship requires more sacrifices for the other. This is possible only when we have true respect and regard for our friends / family members. Friendship is, sometimes, at stake over love affairs. But the true friend always makes sacrifices for friends. It is rightly said that a friend in need is a friend indeed. We are lucky to have about 50 year old friendships with 2-3 old friends.

We can make our family or our near and dear ones very happy by giving due regard and respect to our

spouse and taking care of each other. I am habitual in advising newly married couples with one thoughtful sentence while offering them bouquets and gifts. 'If the husband loses temper even on his mistake, the wife is to keep silent and when the wife loses temper on any issue, then the husband will keep silent'. Sort out the problem amicably after the storm is over. Most of the problems are due to ego and communication gaps. Don't have ego for the happiness of the family. Keep communicating with patience even on contrasting views.

Do we ever remember the day when we offered flowers to our sweet heart? Did we congratulate our darling on getting a promotion? Do we take her / him over for dinner at least on weekends? Do we ever praise our spouse for preparing a delicious lunch or dinner? Do we praise our kids on getting average marks in class? Have we ever tried to find reasons for poor performance of our ward in school? Do we really devote enough time with our kids? Do we treat our kids as our friends and often listen to them with attention in case of distress? Do we really hug our children at least twice a day while sending them to school and after returning from school? If our response is yes, then we are a joyful family. Happiness is prevailing at our home and both of us and our children may be leading happy lives.

Respect for parents, elders, teachers, colleagues in office and respect for our children, employees or subordinate staff and people around us can definitely make us more joyful, free from

unnecessary worries and tensions to have a sound sleep. Sound sleep is one of the essential factors for good health. 7-8 hours of sound sleep clubbed with a balanced diet keeps our blood pressure normal. Happiness and healthy living are interconnected. If we remain happy, we will remain very healthy, since a happy mind resides in a healthy body. Respect to all is thus another attribute for leading a joyful and healthy life.

1. Bow down before God in the home temple before leaving for school / college/ office and convey thanks to God for everything.

2. Say good morning with a smile to our peers in school, college or office. Realize change in mind.

3. By touching the feet of teachers, parents and elderly people, we get their blessings for our long life, good health, prosperity and happiness. We really feel happy after this simple act. Let's try and find the change.

CHAPTER - 5
PASSION FOR WORK

Since our childhood, we all brothers and our lone sister developed the habit of hard work from our both parents. We saw our mother always getting up early in the morning before Sunrise, singing a few songs in honor of God, cleaning the house and preparing us for our village school, when our father was busy running a grocery shop in the nearby town. Mother used to bring water from the nearby well, wash our clothes herself and prepare three meals for the whole family, and did every job with perfection and happiness. All family chores had become her daily routine and she performed them with perfection. We also saw her knitting sweaters for us during the winter season. Seeing her working the whole day, but not tired at all as work had become her passion, which we realized later after growing as adults and started understanding the importance of hard and systematic work. We may follow the following equation for a successful and happy life:

$$\text{Success} = \frac{\text{Luck} \times \text{Systematic Approach}}{\text{Confusion}}$$

The above equation highlights the importance of systematic approach, which is only possible when we love our job, work very hard following different principles of the system i.e. we get engrossed in our work with madness and having least confusion. If we work systematically with least confusion or no confusion then, luck will also help us by grace of God. This is true in every walk of our life. We may have seen many such teachers, who were passionate about their teaching, many doctors, who work for 36 hours during their training period, soldiers of different countries during their strenuous training, engineers working day in and day out for months together to complete huge projects, who are always lost in their work for hours and hours together. Researchers busy in experiments have to forego their lunch or dinner many times, while setting optimum conditions for best results. If we happen to visit railway counters, we may see counter officials working non-stop in dealing with their customers for berths booked for their destinations and same is the case with people working in banks, post offices or any other office of public dealing. All of them love their jobs and due to this love, they develop passion for their work.

We may find many examples of such persons who really become mad after their job. After passing B.Sc. in 1st division (a prestigious position at that time) in 1966 from Hindu College, Sonipat affiliated to Panjab University, I joined the Chemistry Department of Kurukshetra University. Prof. Mukherjee, inventor of the Colonze Mukerjee reaction, was heading the Chemistry department. The department had 26 faculty members including Prof. Mukherjee as professor, 10 readers (Associate Professors) and 15 lecturers (Assistant Professors). All were having great credentials to their credit and were masters of their subject. Prof Mukherjee was a great scholar of his subject and used to teach us advanced topics of organic chemistry. He was considered a very strict administrator besides being a very popular teacher and a high order of researcher. One day, after taking our last class of our batch in 1968, he blessed us with one sentence that, whatever you do, do with passion. He roared in the class with a forceful voice, "You may be an excellent teacher, excellent researcher, very brave army man, excellent officer, excellent clerk, excellent officer, excellent farmer or an excellent dacoit, which made us all have a big laugh".

Prof. Mukherjee's words always kept flashing in my mind and whatever I did, I did with excellence and passion. After joining as a lecturer in chemistry (Assistant Professor) in Hindu College of Panjab University in 1968, switched over to Delhi Administration in 1973 and later joined NCERT in 1975 from where I retired as Prof. of Chemistry in 2007. Besides my very active involvement with my subject as a teacher and as a researcher in Chemistry, I also preferred to work with children living in slums and rural areas of Non-Formal education (NFE), one of the priority schemes of the Govt. of India. Whatever task was assigned to me by higher authorities of NCERT or Ministry of Human Resource Development (MHRD), I always performed my duties of any kind, with love and passion. I always tried with full zeal and enthusiasm and excelled everywhere making me a person with a positive attitude with happiness and good health.

We may come across many people, who are never satisfied with their job. They start criticizing the boss, their colleagues and the system around them. Such persons develop frustration and negativity in their life. They can never be happy, but can remain happy and cheerful by sharing their problems with their colleagues and friends, which may help them to come out of the negative trap of their mind. Even if we feel ourselves overqualified for the present job, and better than our senior, we should try to perform with devotion and dedication with love to our job. We may keep trying for a better job as per our qualification without blaming anyone. When we took up the job, this was our decision. In such a situation, the only solution is to do well in the company of friends or coworkers, but with constant thinking for vertical mobility in that office / company or in some other company. If we keep thinking negatively, we will be a frustrated member of the community and will never be a happy man, which may be detrimental to our own health and for our office and for the Nation. Taking our job as our religion, caring and sharing with friends or colleagues can make us happy.

Passion of Arjun, one of the main characters of Mahabharat may be worthwhile to readers. Arjun had a passion for archery. There was only one competitor to Arjun at that time. He was Karan, but he forgot his skill due to the curse of sage Parshuram, a great warrior of his time, for deceiving him. Those interested may go through the story of Mahabharat. Arjun got a chance to attend one function, where swayamvar (choice of husband by bride's own will) of Draupadi, daughter of King Darupad was held. Arjun with his four brothers Yudhister, Bhim, Nakul and Sahdev and mother Kunti were on their exile for 13 years by deceitful acts of Duryodhan and others.

Condition of Swayamvar was to hit the eye of the rotating fish by seeing her reflection down in the pan containing oil. Arjun, after stretching his bow, aimed at the eye only and succeeded in hitting the eye of the fish. Arjun's passion for archery helped him to marry Draupadi and win the fiercest battle of Mahabharat by killing all Kaurvas and hundreds of thousands of warriors on Kauravas' side. Such is the importance of passion for the job.

My own story may be helpful to those, who don't find them better placed or take the job much below their qualifications, not feeling happy being away from their homes. I got a class 1 post as a lecturer in chemistry in Hindu college in my own town just after passing M.Sc. in first division, with a merit position. In college I was very happy to take my theory class in the morning and practical classes in the afternoon after enjoying lunch with my wife and parents. I used to enjoy going to the college by walking and sometimes by having a cycle ride. We were 25 lecturers in the chemistry department of Hindu college with my position number 12 in the seniority list at that time.

In the early seventies, students started preferring commerce streams than science. Thus the number of science students kept decreasing every year. The same happened with the fate of the teaching faculty of science stream. The college management started retrenching science faculty members in the beginning of every academic year and after three years, I was also retrenched by handing over three months' salary along with the retrenchment notice due to the fall in strength of science students. The news of retrenchment was like a bolt from the blue to me and to our joint family. But I never gave up. I filed a case against the management in the university and won the case. Eventually after a struggle of about three years in Delhi administration, I succeeded in getting a class 1 post again in NCERT – A National level organization looking after school education in India.

During my tenure of 32 years in NCERT, I learnt a lot about pedagogy of teaching while teaching chemistry to undergraduate students. I learnt about new techniques of teaching, preparing better teachers by making use of microteaching – a technique adopted from Stanford University by NCERT in 1976. I tried my hands in the new thrust areas as per priorities of Government of India (GOI) for Universalisation of Elementary Education (UEE). Non-Formal Education (NFE) was not my area but the principal made me coordinator of this new scheme seeing my enthusiasm and passion for teaching. NFE was for children not going to schools as they had to stay at home to look after their siblings at home or accompany their parents to fields to supplement the family income. Working in different activities besides our main job, makes us more happy and joyful with more learning.

This is possible only when we enjoy our every job and develop a passion for it. My experience in NFE in the country was well recognized by the authorities both at the state level and central government level. The District Primary Education Program (DPEP) project was going on in India to raise the literacy level with the help of European countries. Teams of European countries were visiting different states of India for critical appraisal of the NFE program going on in different states of India. To my pleasant surprise, I was asked by MHRD to join the World Bank team as a representative of GOI for Gujarat state, in spite of being a man of chemistry. This could be possible only by accepting all tasks assigned to me with love and passion, but without neglecting my main subject area of chemistry. If I published one paper in NFE or science/chemistry education, I did publish one paper in chemistry too. I was the only research guide in two subjects i.e. chemistry and education in the university. Adam Grant (11) in his bestselling book "Think Again" also emphasizes on shifting job / business from time to time to be a successful entrepreneur, but after having knowledge of all the pros and cons of the other assignment.

Besides academic activities, I was helping the administration in various co - curricular activities of the college, which kept me always busy from morning till night at my college and at home taking care of my wife and three growing children. Children learn from homes, from their parents and the home atmosphere. Parents are said to be the first teachers and we paid full attention to their development. Our three children started learning the value of time, punctuality, regards to teachers, elders and peers, and not postponing the task for the next day. They remained diligent from the very beginning and now are doing extremely well in their own fields at different places in different countries, which always keeps us healthy and happy. Husband and wife are just like two wheels of the chariot to keep excellent balance. My wife always proved better than me in every aspect-extending me a helping hand by joining some English medium school as an English teacher, but also taking care of the family with full devotion. She always loved school jobs and daily home chores with passion. She left no stone unturned to inculcate family values in our children namely respecting all, punctuality, diligence, love and passion for their school activities besides academics and caring and sharing their lunch boxes with their class fellows, which they are following till date with their friends and colleagues. We feel proud to find them very social and always helping their friends or colleagues.

There are thousands of people in the world who work constantly throughout their life to bring cheers to fellow beings or people at large spread throughout the world by their unending efforts for new inventions to make life more comfortable. The list may be very long but Arya Bhatt, who gave the concept of zero to the world, Lord Krishna who preached the concept of Karma (duty consciousness) to the world through his disciple Arjun, James Watt who developed the first steam engine to bring industrial revolution, Thomas Edison inventor of incandescent light bulb, motion picture camera, and improving the telegraph and telephone, Martin King Luther Jr. for fighting for civil rights of black people in America, Mahatma Gandhi for fighting against racial discrimination in South Africa and later for getting freedom for India from the clutches of England by non- violence means, Indira Gandhi for liberating East Bengal from Pakistan and bringing happiness on faces of millions of people of Bangladesh after surrender of more than 92,000 army men of Pakistan, will be remembered forever.

Last 50 years are credited to Information Technology, when many new inventions have taken place for making the lives of trillions of people more and more comfortable by new electronic gadgets in the market of both developing and developed countries. Computers, laptops, cordless phones (mobiles), smart phones, iPhones have changed the lifestyle of people all over the globe. This could be possible only by the constant and concerted efforts of the visionary Steve Jobs (12) who had the passion for electronics. This was during the tenure of interim chairmanship of Steve Jobs that the first Apple computer came in the market and then his constant thinking for cordless mobile phones bought the iphone and ipad which brought a tremendous change in human life. The Contributions of Bill Gates, Mark Zukerberg, Jan Koum and Brian Acton, who invented WhatsApp in 2009 former employees of Yahoo, brought revolution in the IT Industry, which proved a milestone in human history.

WhatsApp and Facebook have brought the world very close to each other. All of us are now very much dependent on these inventions in our daily life. World has become very fast and very small. These electronic gadgets have brought cheers on our faces but overuse has made our life very terrible too. If we want to lead a joyful and healthy life, we will have to reduce screen time for a joyful and healthy life. According to the NBC news, Warren Buffet (13), the fourth wealthiest person in the world and CEO of Berkshire Hathaway, didn't own a mobile phone till last year. There are 10 other extremely successful people in the world who don't use technology. This is up to us how to lead an uncomfortable or comfortable living on earth.

Some of us may be running our own business or working as an employee of any level in any company, two simple words of love and passion can make us a successful entrepreneur. But love and passion for the job never come automatically. This comes from core values of honesty, sincerity, loyalty with a little bit of creativity, intelligence and above all diligence. Failures and falling in the ditches are the best teachers. If we care for our employees both at good and bad times treating them well, their colleagues and family members, they will always be ready to take the company to the pinnacle of glory and never ditch in distress. Hire and fire have become very common in some companies, but such companies always prove losers in the long run. Tatas and Birlas may not be the topmost companies, but they are the most respected and known for transparent business with highest credibility level in India and abroad as well. We may find many teachers, doctors, engineers, scientists, technocrats, bureaucrats, defense personnel and persons working in many more fields around us who command high respect in their own fields not only by virtue of excellence in their field, but also for passion for their jobs.

Hence, passion for our job plays an extremely important role in every field for the success stories around us and to lead a joyful and healthy life.

1. Resolve something before starting the day and see to it how far we accomplished that.

2. Make a diary and start writing daily activities with failures by now.
3. Never give up in spite of failures. keep thinking fresh and divergently.
4. Never remain in the box. Try to do something new and silly. No idea isa silly idea.
5. Never share a plan before taking that to the final destination.
6. Make full use of 24 hours by time management.

CHAPTER – 6
LOVE FOR ALL, STRESSES & DEVELOPMENTS

The word 'love' is the opposite of 'hatred'. Hatred leads to chaos, troubles, unhappiness, physical and mental stresses to people, whereas love brings harmony, happiness, peace, good physical and mental health and a beautiful ambience around us. Love is not only between persons of opposite sex or same sex, love can be between father and son, brothers, sisters, teacher and students, employer and employee, house owner and domestic helpers, between CEO of a company and the workforce. It's very common when people express love for their community members, their town, their state and above all their nation, positive vibes start flowing in our body. The United Nations Organization was established after World War II in 1945 to avoid conflict and bring harmony between 51 founding member states and now 193 sovereign nations having contrasting ways of thinking. "Vasudhaiva Kutumbakam" (The whole Earth is our Family) mentioned in Maha Upanishad (14) in Sanskrit thousands of years ago by our sages in India was the theme for the Group of 20 presidency in 2024, when Prime Minister Narendra Modi emphasized that we consider the whole world as one family, where we may live with love and peace. This phrase became the mantra of the diplomatic lexicon. Our sages have been advocating for the welfare of all human beings throughout the globe as depicted in Rigveda (15),

Hindus holy book written by Indian sages on palm leaves some 3500 years ago.

The Holy book RamcharitManas (story of Lord Ram, the incarnation of Lord Vishnu in Hindu mythology) written by Goswami Tulsi Das in 1574 (16), first published in Calcutta (Kolkata now) in 1810, is now published regularly by Geeta Press Gorakhpur in Uttar Pradesh in India. RamcharitManas' book is kept in almost every home of Hindu families. The holy book highlights the love between King Dasratha and his four sons, love of Ram with his own mother and the other two queens of King Dasratha as well, rather more for his youngest mother Kekai, love of Laxman for his elder brother Ram, for whom he left his wife and palace for service of elder brother while leaving the throne and proceeding to forests. The book makes a special mention of the unfailing love of another brother Bharat for Ram, who took care of Ram's throne by putting Ram's sleepers on the throne. Bharat acted as a caretaker of the throne for 14 years but never occupied Ram's chair, contrary to present day litigations going on between brothers and even father and the sons over property issues. The whole scenario is undergoing drastic change over the last 50-60 years. Unbelievable to old timers for such a situation not only in India but in most of the countries.

Love of Sita for her husband Ram is also exemplary when Sita, daughter of the mighty King Janak also left the empire of Ayodhya taking out her princely costumes and precious ornaments gifted to her by King Janak and King Dashratha. Sita went to forests barefooted along with Ram to give her husband company. Those who have not read "Ramcharitmanas" may like to understand the importance of love of Ram for common man residing in forests and respect for scholarly sages during 14 years of forest stay. Ram, Sita and Laxman, also came across many rogues troubling sages in their worships for deities. There is an interesting story of the boatman named Nishadraj asking Ram to allow him to clean his feet before boarding his boat for crossing the Ganges, out of fear that his boat may not turn into a lady like Ahilya after touching her stone statue by Ram. This episode reflects the extreme love of every category of people living in forests. Extreme love and unparalleled wish of Sabri, the tribal woman to meet Ram also forms a very interesting story during their stay in Jungle. On seeing Ram, Laxman and Sita on the doorstep of her hutt, Sabri started tasting fruits around her before offering to Ram. Ram accepted those fruits before tasted by Sabri without any hesitation respecting the love of the devotee for him.

Ram, Sita and Lxman also met many wretched fellows in forests, who used to trouble the innocent tribal people and gave them relief by making forests free from such antisocial elements. During the 14th year of exile of Ram, the crooked lady srurpanakha, sister of Ravana, the super powerful king of Lanka happened to come across handsome Ram and Laxman near their cottage in the forest and started pressing both of them to marry her. She became the real culprit for the war between Ram and the mighty Ravana,but that proved a blessing in disguise for the tribal people and sages who used to worship their deities daily, but villains like, Mareech, Ahiravan, Meghnath, Kumbhkaran and Ravana, the scholarly but the greatest rogue of his time and all others such anti social elements were killed by Ram and Laxman with the help of Lord Hanuman, Sugreev, Vibhheshan, the right thinking younger brother of Ravana and many other residents of forests. After Killing Ravana, his all sons and his army men, Laxman brought Sita back from Ashok Vatika and handed over the throne of Lanka to Vibheeshan.

There are many learning points if we go through RamcharitManas with faith and by understanding every version in Awadhi language with translation in Hindi, English and many other languages, we will come across where we find the stories of love and respect for Ram and by Ram for those whomsoever he met in forests during the exile of 14 years. The love of Ram for Nishadraj is also exemplary to accede to his request to let him wash his feet before boarding the boat. Ram never used the authority as the son of king Dashrath, in contrast to the pride and authoritarian attitude of present day novice politicians in Asia and other countries. Love of Ram for birds was also unique, when he stopped to take care of the dying vulture, Jatayu, on the ground while going in search of Sita. Ram went ahead only after performing the last rites of Jatayu. By not accepting the offer of beautiful Shrupankha for marriage, Ram showed his utmost love and respect for sita and he never believed in polygamy, though his father had three queens. If Sugreev had developed friendship with Ram on the advice of Hanuman, Ram kept his promise by getting Sugreev rid of his elder brother Bali, who pushed out

Sugree from his empire without his wife. Sugreev was made the king again by Ram.

Hanuman's resolve of crossing over the Indian Ocean in a single lap is a lesson for us that we should never give up and never delay things by putting off our plans. Once resolved, we should fight with full force and our utmost mental and physical power and rest not till the goal is achieved. Such a resolve always leads us to success to make us happy and healthy.

Ram had patience and never lost temper even with his enemies except at one stage, when the Indian ocean didn't come forward to show the way to Ram's Army for crossing over the huge sea. Ram's regard for Ravana, his foe who committed the heinous crime of kidnapping his wife, has been exemplary when Ram sent Laxman to the dying Ravana to listen to his advice keeping in view scholarliness of the mighty king, though he had committed a heinous crime.

Ram left for Ayodhya along with wife Sita, Laxman, Vibhishan, Sugreev, Hanuman in Pushpak Viman (the special Aircraft of Ravana) followed by the Vanar Sena to meet his younger brothers Bharat and Shatrughan, mothers, ministers, sages, and the citizens who had been waiting to welcome them for the last 14 years. They reached Ayodhya on the 15th day of Kartik month (October - November of Hindu calendar). The whole Ayodhya was decorated like a beautiful bride glittering with lights of lamps. This day is celebrated as DIWALI in India and many other countries by Hindus besides people of many faiths, when everyone celebrates the festival as one's own.

There is another holy book of Hindus named Bhagwat Geeta (17) describing the story of mutual love of five Pandavas (sons of King Pandu) following the righteous path under the guidance of Lord Krishna (another incarnation of Lord Vishnu) and 101 Kauravas (sons of King Dhritarashtra- blind by birth) having evil designs always against their cousins. After defeating Pandavas in gambling under the treacherous plans of their maternal uncle Shakuni, Kaurvas went to exile for 12 years. After finishing their exile when Pandvas reached indraprastha, kaurvas refused to give even 5 villages to five Pandavas as suggested by Lord Krishna. So there was no alternative except the battle. Before the start of the battle, Kaurvas requested Krishna to hand over His army to them, but Pandvas requested Krishna to be on their side just to guide them without any weapon in His hand. Huge forces on both sides assembled in the battlefield of Kurukshetra for the fight. Bhishma Pitamaha had to accept commandership of Kauvas forces due to his promise to be on the side of the King. Krishna accepted to be the driver of Arjun's Chariot. When Krishna took the chariot of Arjun in the battlefield, Arjun went into depression to see his grandfather Bhisma and his cousins Kaurvas with whom he was to fight and kill them or be killed by them. The thought of guilt of winning the battle by killing his own brethren and grandfather Bhishma and his teacher Dronacharya penetrated in his mind and body. Arjun threw his Gandiv dhanush (Bow) and arrows and refused to fight with the army of Kauravas. Arjun asked Krishna to take him away from the battlefield. This was at this stage that Lord

Krishna took Arjun's chariot on one side and gave him a sermon to act without thinking of consequences as described in the Holy Book "BhagwatGeeta".

Sermons of Lord Krishna to Arjun in the battle field are compiled as, "Bhagwat Geeta," a holy book worth reading not only for Hindus but for everyone all over the globe. The book is available in Sanskrit, Hindi, English and many other languages. Worth reading for all. The main crux of Bhawat Geeta is – 'keep doing work assigned to you with full vigor, determination and full sincerity without caring for the result, which is always in the hands of The Almighty'.

If we get a chance to read Bhagwat Geeta or the story of Mahabharat (The Furious Battle) fought between forces of Pandavas and Kaurvas at the battlefield of Kurukshetra in Haryana state of India from 23 October to 9 November 900 BCE (18) some more than 2900 years ago, we will find many characters of love and respect for each other and hatred too due to zealous nature among cousins, which has become very common now. All five Pandvas namely Yudhishtar, Bheem, Arjun, Nakul and Sahdev had unparalleled love for each other, high regard for their mother Kunti, their advisor Krishna, who was their cousin and always well wisher of all. They had high regard for their grandfather Bhishma and their sage teacher Dronacharya though they were fighting on behalf of their cousins Kaurvas.

Gambling between kings and princes was in vogue at that time too. Kaurvas invited their cousins Pandavas to stay with them at their place for sometime. Not understanding the evil designs of Duryodhan, the oldest son of Dharitrashtra, Pandavas agreed to play gambling with them. But they lost everything due to the cheating strategies of Shakuni, maternal uncle of Kauravas. As per agreement, Pandavas had to leave their kingdom with their mother Kunti and wife Draupdi by leaving all property and even personal belongings. They were asked to remain in forests for 12 years with last year in Agyatwas (in hidden state and not to be recognised by anyone).

Their mother Kunti loved all her sons equally and used to ask them to distribute whatever they had from the forest after the daylong efforts in search of daily meals which they used to take together with mother in the evening. There is an interesting story of their agyatvas during the last year. Once all brothers happened to enter the Panchal Kingdom of the mighty king Drupad, also known as Yajneshna (he whose army is sacrificial) and found some swayamvar (marriage by the will of the bride) taking place as per condition stated in earlier chapter. Arjun participated in the competition without revealing his identity and succeeded in hitting the eye of the rotating fish. Arjun took Draupadi along with his four brothers and told their mother for today's earnings. The mother without having a look on Draupadi asked her sons to distribute themselves as usual. An embarrassing situation was created by the unbelievable sentence of their mother but all five brothers agreed to be Draupdi's husband by keeping her with every brother for one month by rotation..

There are a few great lessons from the above episode for all of us that we should never gamble and think before speaking. Moreover, we shouldn't be blind followers of anyone. Sometimes, we believe our family members and friends so much that we sign important documents without reading, which can be very harmful to us in the long run.

Pandvas had huge respect for their uncle King Dhritrashtra, father of Kauravas but due to his unfailing love for his eldest son Duryodhan and other 100 sons, he never showed unbiased attitude towards Pandavas. His actions were always biased. He never stopped Duryodhan from organizing gambling games with Pandavas, due to which they lost everything, insulting Draupadi in the palace courtyard in presence of all elderly persons of the family. Duryodhan and his brothers always made plans to kill pandavas, once even trying to burn them in Lakshagraha (palace made of lacquer), but were saved by the efforts of Prime Minister Vidur. If there are incidents of extreme love among them and unfailing regard for their grandfather and Krisna, the Mahabharata epic is full of characters of hatred, deceits and their zealous nature, which became the root cause of total destruction of the family or even the most powerful state of any country. Russian president Putin has hatred for Ukrainians, and Israeli Prime Minister Benjamin Ntanyahu has for palestinians. Very difficult to say who is right and who is wrong.

Let's learn to live with peace with love and affection for all around us keeping the old slogan, 'Live and Let others live'.

It would be worthwhile here to narrate another interesting story of honesty and duty consciousness of King Harishchandra and his wife who never budged an inch from honesty, when Harishchandra (19) didn't agree to perform cremation of his own son without charging the cremation fee from her wife, who had no alternative but got ready to take off her clothes as the cremation fee as she was having nothing else with her.

Satya Harishchandra was the great grandfather of Dashratha, the king of Ayodhya. He was the 33rd descendent of the Iksvaku family. Once upon a time, the king decided to go hunting accompanied by his ministers and biggule blowers. Sage Vishvamitra engaged in meditation was disturbed by ears hurting sounds of biggule blowers. On being disturbed by the unwanted noise, the sage opened his eyes and found the peripheral of king Harishchandra's procession passing through the forest. The sage asked the king to stop and cursed him to strip from his kingdom and also asked him to pay 1000 gold coins to the sage within one month as the penalty, but by working outside his kingdom.

Harishchandra started a job in the neighboring state with a very low wage. After working for 2-3 days, the king understood that he wouldn't be able to earn 1000 gold coins within one month. The King sold himself, his wife and 5 years old son Rohitashvwa to a Chandal (the person carrying out cremation), who agreed to pay him 1000 gold coin after completion of one month but he will have to perform his duty at the cremation ground all the 24 hours, and charging fee from relatives of dead person and deposit the gold coins to him daily. Once Harishchandra's wife Shiva went to the garden to pick flowers, but his son Rohitashva standing by the side of his mother was bitten by a snake and he died (20). Harishchandra's wife took her son for burial (children under 16 years of age are not cremated) and found her husband performing cremations of dead bodies. On her turn, Shiva handed over the body to her husband, but Harishchandra asked her to pay tax for burial of the body of his own son. Shiva, not having any gold coin with her, offered to pay a piece of her only saree (the cloth wrapped around their body by ladies at that time in Asian countries), which she was wearing in lieu of the tax. Seeing the duty of the husband and the wife, the sage Visvamitra appeared on the scene and stopped Shiva to tear her saree. Being impressed by the honesty of Harishchandra and his wife Shiva, the sage freed them from his curse and asked them to return to their kingdom along with their son Rohitashva, after bringing him back to life. Both Harishchandra and his wife loved each other and the wife never asked her husband to deviate from the path of his duty even at the cost of prestige of his wife.

We should always perform our duty with love, passion, honesty and consciousness without being swayed away by materialistic things around us.

Old family systems of India and many other countries are really praiseworthy, when most of them used to live in a joint family. Children and grandchildren used to live together with their parents, cousins, grandparents and sometimes even great grandparents with love, affection and regards for the elders. They used to enjoy the sense of social security under the supervision of elderly persons of the family besides inculcating social values like caring and sharing, respect for elders and love for the youngers, and life values like social etiquettes, punctuality, truthfulness, respect to teachers and elderly persons of the community and helping the needy persons. In my own family, I was brought up under the patronage of my grandmother, parents, and my elder brother along with my four younger brothers and one sister. During summer vacations we used to go to our home town with three children namely Bobby (pankaj), Gudia(Kavita) and Dolly (deepika) and our younger brother CPG also used to join us from Lucknow with his wife and three children namely Guddu(Pratibha), Bharat and Nitu. At one stage there used to be more than 20 persons under one umbrella with a common kitchen living very happily, dining together after the daylong activities of all individuals, doing our school/college homework, helping the younger members and sitting around the bed of our father to listen to his very interesting stories at night. Those days were the golden days of love, happiness, carefree life and no worries. School and college going children were disciplined in school and outside with no complaint from any member of the society, unlike the present incidents of fights, molestation, rape and murders and anxieties all around us by youths.

Situation has totally changed in India and other countries as well. The joint family system has become very rare due to developments taking place in every field of the society. Literacy rate in India has shown a great improvement from just 16 percent in 1947 to 77.7 percent in 2023 (21) with an increase of population from 340 M in 1947 to 1.441B in 2024 (22) by opening more Sr. Secondary schools, colleges and universities in all states of progressing India. Infrastructure has improved a lot by connecting far flung areas of the country by road, rail and air. Roads, rail tracks and air connectivity has increased tremendously during the last 75 years (23). Roads length increased from 0.2M km in 1947 to 6.33M km and National Highways to 2M km in 2023-4. The similar increasing trend is observed in rail tracks, which increased from 55,000 km in 1947 to 129,000 km in 2023-24. Number of railway stations has increased to 8,000, which is the highest in the world. 11B passengers traveled by Indian railways in 2023-24 and 1.416B tonnes of freight was carried by railways in the same year. These developments are bringing more shine to the faces of people living in far flung areas with an increase of their per capita income thus making them more healthy and happy.

First Metro in India was started on 24 October, 1984 in Calcutta (now known as Kolkata). The second one was Delhi Metro, becoming functional on December 24, 2002 controlling the traffic congestion of Delhi. Many more metros have now started in different capital cities. The fast running Vande Bharat trains have been introduced in India during the last five years. The first Vande Bharata train was started between New Delhi and Varanasi on 18 Feb., 2019 (24). Many more are now running from different capital cities. Number of airports and the passengers traveling from 486 domestic and international airports of India has increased tangentially to 154M (25) in 2023-24.

These developments look very eye-catching but they have disturbed the old culture of Indians, who used to live very happily with their family members with minimums. People living in huts and villages with minimum material at their level, are found to lead a happy and carefree life by working very hard during the day and free from very common diseases like hypertension and diabetes with their counterparts living in big towns and cities. With establishment of new industries in the nearby towns and cities, youths have started migrating from their homes in rural areas to nearby towns and cities in search of jobs. Though they keep visiting their home places quite frequently, they prefer to settle at places near to their job center. Another very positive development is girls' education with upward trends in recent years due to which both partners have started looking for jobs for better living in cities. These developments have led to the shift from joint families to nuclear families. Parents keep visiting their children, but they can't stay permanently with their children due to liabilities at their own home town to look after their cattle, agriculture and other activities. These developments are responsible for erosion of family values leading to more worries, anxieties, tensions and unhappiness in a large number of families of big cities. People living at small places with minimums are still found to be happier than their counterparts living in big cities with modern amenities of all kinds.

There is a need to open small industries related to agriculture or their produce grown at the local level, senior secondary schools, and public health centers at block level to provide jobs to the youth and health facilities to the public so that they can live with their parents and can lead a happier life.

Would we like to think of the following attributes to make us healthy and happy?

1. Do we live with our parents? If not, do we visit them very often or call them regularly?

2. Do we spare time to join them on happy and shocking incidents?

3. Do we care for our elderly family members by taking care of their needs regularly?

4. Do we care for our domestic help by offering a cup of tea off and on, and do we ever contribute for the birthday of their children? Do we help them in distress?

5. Have we had one or two old friends for the last 30 years? If yes, we are a very happy person.

6. Do we visit the houses of our domestic help during their good days and times of distress ? If yes, we are a happy family.

CHAPTER-7
NATION FIRST REST NEXT

Loving and happy family members make our community happy, and happy community members make township happy. Happy towns or cities make our district or our state happy, ultimately making a happy Nation. India and China are the two most populous countries not only of Asia but that of the world. However, these are not the top happiest countries; rather find a very back seat in the list of happy countries. Finland with a small population of 5.5M, per capita income of US $50,836 is the happiest country as mentioned earlier but we are placed much behind our neighboring countries namely Nepal, Bhutan, Bangladesh and the mighty China. The reason may be obvious due to overpopulation, diversity of culture, customs, language and many religions. This may be true to some extent, but diversity of India is making our Nation great because Indians of all religions speaking different languages with different customs are hard core nationalists and majority of them consider their Nation first in all eventualities.

Fremont city of California in the US is the happiest city of America, with one contributing factor of having the highest share of households with an income of $75,000, at nearly 80%. Industrial city Kanpur of Uttar Pradesh is found the happiest city in India with 40th position of happy cities of the world, followed by the Pink City Jaipur in Rajasthan, Chennai,

Mangalore, Mysuru, Hyderabad, Pune and Chandigarh (26), reason being of excellent law and order, better education, more job and business opportunities in these cities and their peripheries, but surprisingly leaving behind the capital city of New Delhi. Thousands and thousands of people commute to Delhi from nearby satellite NCR (National Capital Region) towns daily by traveling more than 100 km from their homes and back by many connecting trains from all directions. Day of such commuters starts at 4.00 am and after daily duty of more than 10 hours in ministry offices / private organizations etc., they reach home by 10.00 pm or so. Thus they have to devote more than 6 hours in trains to reach their place of work and then back to home late in the night, thus making such people unhappy in the capital city of Delhi. But they are determined to work for their families, communities and ultimately their Nation to keep marching ahead. I myself had to face the same experience of commuting and working for more than 18 hours a day during my struggling period of three years in early seventies for my vertical mobility and above all for the happiness of my family.

There are many examples of people working in different fields for the betterment of their country with firm conviction, devotion, dedication, loyalty and patriotism in their mind. 70 percent of the population of India lives in villages with agriculture as the main profession. Farmers are the backbone of the agricultural economy of any Nation. The farmers start their day early in the morning for going out to their fields for watering the growing plants, to plough the fields with bullocks (some 70 years ago), but now with tractors and sowing of seeds along with their women folk, then taking care of buffalos, cows, bullocks, camels etc in milking and feeding them twice a day. During the harvesting season, they are to work throughout the day in scorching heat, with sweat flowing from their lean and thin body but the chorus folk songs of their areas by the ladies in their fields always keep them and the men folk not lagging behind their counterparts in terms of good health and cheerfulness.

The youths of every country make their Nation proud by winning medals in games and sports at different levels. Indian sportspersons (both male and female) have also made India proud by winning medals in different Olympics, commonwealth games and other national and international games and sports tournaments (27). Indian players have been in the race in winning gold, silver and bronze medals since 1900. Norman Pritchard was the first Indian to earn a silver medal in the Men's 200 meter hurdles race at Paris. Major Dhyan Chand, popularly known as Hockey Wizard and his teammates won gold medals in hockey in 1928 at Amsterdam, in 1932 at Los Angeles and in 1936 at Berlin and continued in following Olympics with some intermittent intervals. Many Indian players won many individual medals in boxing, wrestling, weight lifting, shooting etc. making us proud – Wrestler K.D. Jadhav was the first Indian to win individual Bronze medal Men's bantamweight wrestling at Helsinki in 1952; Leander Paes won Bronze medal in Men's singles tennis in 1996 and Karnam Malleswari won Bronze medal in Women's 54 kg weightlifting at Sydney Olympic in 2000.

Rajyawardhan Singh Rathore won Silver medal in Men's double trap shooting. Abhinav Bindra was the first winner of gold medal in 10m air rifle shooting in 2008 at Beijing. At the same Olympics, Vijender Singh won the Bronze in Men's middleweight boxing and Sushil KUmar won Bronze in Men's 66kg wrestling.

London Olympic in 2012 was quite rewarding for Indian Olympians, when Sushil Kumar won Silver in Men's 66kg wrestling; Vijay Kumar won Silver in Men's 25 meter rapid pistol shooting; Saina Nehwal with Bronze in Women's singles badminton and Mary Kom with Bronze medal in boxing in 2012 made us proud again. P.V. Sindhu won silver medal in 2016 in Women's singles badminton and Sakshi Malik, the first Indian woman won Bronze in Women's 58kg wrestling in 2016 bringing cheers on faces of not only women folk of the country but all Indians. Bajrang Punia won the gold medal in the commonwealth games in 2017. Many more Indian players made their countrymen happy by winning medals in different games in the last Olympic at Tokyo in 2020. India won 1 Gold; 2 Silver; and 4 Bronze medals in different events at Tokyo Olympics. Neeraj Chopra won Gold medal Men's javelin throw; Mirabi Chanu got Silver medal in Women's 49 kg weightlifting; Raj Kumar Dahiya got Silver in Men's 57 kg wrestling and P.V. Sindhu won Bronze in badminton (singles). Lovlina Borgohain brought laurels to India by winning Bronze in Women's welterweight boxing, and another Bronze medal by the Indian hockey team. Bajrang Punia won Bronze in Men's 65 kg wrestling thus making India proud and making all Indians a much happier lot at Tokyo Olympics. Indian players won one silver medal and five bronze at the Paris Olympics in 2024, but differently abled players made all Indians and the country proud by winning 29 medals in Para- Olympic at Paris including seven Gold, nine silver, and 13 bronze breaking all records.

There are thousands and thousands of our young players (both men and women) in many other international events of games and sports, who are entertaining youths and citizens of all ages all over the globe and making them happy by their achievements. Cricket is such a game played in every street of rural and urban India by children, youths and men and women of all ages displaying a lot of hustle and bustle around us during the days and nights, making our youths healthy and happy and enhancing the prestige of India by winning world cups. The memory of winning the ODI World Cup (EST. 1975) by the Indian team in 1983 (28) under the stewardship of young and dashing captain Kapil Deo is very fresh in the minds of the generation of eighties. Eight teams participated in the final match between Indian and the mighty West Indies team at Lord's stadium in England. The second time India won the ODI world cup under the captainship of M.S. Dhoni brought unparallel vibes in all Indians from children of 5 years of age till 90 years old in 2011 by defeating Sri Lanka by six wickets with Gutam Gambhir at 97 and Dhoni at 91 not out. We Indians are fans of cricket and watching live cricket matches make all Indians very happy and happiness leads to good physical and mental health making the nation proud of their players by their untiring efforts for the country.

Players when free from do regular practice in stadiums to keep them fit and uptodate for the upcoming national events. They take proper diets and do regular exercise for their good health, keeping them happy and fit at the stadiums. The same is true for players of other countries as well throughout the world without any barriers or taboos of any kind. T20 World Cup 2024 was co-hosted by the West Indies and the United States in June 2024 and India won the world cup in the last ball by defeating the mighty team of South Africa making the countrymen proud when there was an electric charge in the whole stadium, where thousands of Iandians started dancing by the unparalleled win. 20 teams participated in the world cup, with the US participating for the first time.

"Health is Wealth" is the motto for children, youths and the elderly persons throughout the world because a sound mind rests in a sound body to keep us Healthy and Happy.

The same feeling of working with zeal, enthusiasm, devotion, dedication and sincerity to work and loyalty to their organization is exhibited by employees working in different sectors of society - some working in the public sector and many others working in corporate offices of big companies. If 20 percent of the employees happen to be shirkers, the majority is that of sincere workers. These are the intelligent, diligent, devoted and loyal employees, who make any nation great and their countrymen by their hard work, creative thinking with a healthy body and a happy brain. If we start thinking that every human being contributes to the development of the nation, without pinpointing their shortcomings, things will start improving. We must try to uplift the standard of poor people to get real happiness. This is the human weakness that everyone needs respect and appreciation. If we start using positive reinforcement techniques after any positive happening, there would be happiness around us. We will remain happy and there may be more vibes of happiness and positive energy around us. By reading stories of great politicians, great teachers, great freedom fighters, scientists, doctors, engineers, astronomers and space scientists who made our lives happier by their research work in different fields, we will be highly motivated to do better and even motivate our own children and community members to reach the pinnacle of glory.

All big people were never born with silver spoons in their mouths. Mahatma Gandhi had to struggle a lot in South Africa after being thrown out from the first class coach of the train even with the first class train ticket due to racial discrimination. Gandhi kept sitting on the platform after being kicked out of the train. There he started the right for equality without any coerciveness, but fighting for his right by non-violence means in South Africa. This technique of non - violence helped Gandhi and thousands and thousands of freedom fighters of congress irrespective of their caste and creed and many other parties to get freedom for India from the yolk of England in 1947. There is a great lesson of "United we stand< divided we fall" in the freedom movement. Freedom brought happiness and glitters to the struggling Indians living in small villages, towns and big cities in different parts of India after facing various kinds of oppressions by the British crown. India became a democratic country by following three pillars of Secularism, socialism and democracy. This is just one example. Gandhi became synonymous with freedom without violence against the rulers.

Dr. Martin Luther King Jr. was a great follower of Gandhi and he succeeded in abolishing the slavery system in America. Nelson Mandela fought for freedom of South Africa again by adopting non-violence means. These are examples of individuals, besides thousands of freedom fighters in their own countries who brought happiness on the faces of their fellows. We may find many more such examples in different countries where some right thinking people are fighting for civil liberties for their people by undergoing imprisonment and getting oppressed by the mighty and egoistic rulers in many counties. Indian Forces helped the freedom fighters of Eastern Pakistan (now Bangladesh) to get them freedom from the brutal forces of Pakistan and brought cheers on the faces of millions of freedom fighters of Bangladesh. But such egoistic and brutal rulers can never be happy. They would have the guilt of their wrong doings or they will commit suicide like the mighty Hitler.

Teachers are other community members, who have been the fulcrum of bringing change in the society by changing the oppressive rulers by their constant and untiring efforts. Chanakya (29) has been one such Indian polymath (375 – 283 BCE), who was active as a teacher, author, strategist, philosopher, economist, jurist, and politician, who served as the chief advisor to both emperors Chandragupta and his son Bindusar - the two mighty Maurian emperors and teacher of Ashoka, the son of Bindusara. Chanakya is popularly known as Kautilya or Visnugupta , who authored the ancient Indian political treatise, the Arthshastra, a text roughly brought out in the fourth century BCE. As such, Chanakya is considered the pioneer in the field of political science and economics. Around 321 BCE, Chankya assisted the first Mauryan emperor Chandragupta in his rise to power by destroying the Nanda empire by dethroning the most incompetent and oppressive ruler Dhana Nanda of Magadh (30) to bring happiness to citizens of Magadh empire, some 2,300 years ago.

There have been many such examples of great philosophers of their time known for their own principles and firm conviction, who sacrificed their lives without bulging an inch from their thoughts. Socrates (31) was one such Greek philosopher, who was killed by giving him common hemlock poison on Feb. 15, 399 BC. Socrates was respected for his bravery as a soldier, for the patience he showed to his wife, for the kindness he treated children with, and the finally for the restraint he showed when he was sentenced to death for his guilt of two charges – Asebeia (impiety) against the pantheon of Athens, and corruption of the city – state; the accusers cited two impious acts by Socrates: failing to 'acknowledge the gods that the city acknowledges, and introducing new deities. Nicolaus Copernicus, (32) a Polish astronomer, was another scientist to give his theory of revolution of the Earth around the Sun in 1543. Nicolaus's theory, called Copernican heliocentrism, was something unbelievable at that time, as most of the people believed that the Sun, not the Earth, was the center of the Universe. It took over a century for Copernicus's theory to become widely accepted, and later supported by other scientists such as Galileo Galilei (33) and Isaac Newton (34). Thus, happiness can be brought also by teachers, scientists, engineers, astronauts and many others to make life more comfortable by their constant and concerted research in their own fields.

Artists, poets and people of divergent thinking also make people happy by their artistic work. Rabindranath Tagore (35) was awarded the Nobel prize in 1913 in literature "because of his profoundly sensitive, fresh and beautiful verse (translated Geetanjali), by which, with consummate skill, he has made his poetic thought, expressed in his own English words, a part of the literature of the West." Another Indian to get the Nobel Prize in the early twentieth century was Dr. C.V. Raman, FRS (36), who got the Award in 1930 for his discovery on scattering of light on Feb.29, 1928 and for the discovery of the effect named after his name as "Raman Effect". Many other notable Nobel Prize winner, Indians and others, include Har Gobind Khorana (1968) in physiology or medicine; Mother Teresa (1979) for Peace, Subrahmanyan Chandrashekhar (1983) in Physics; Amartya Sen (1998) in Economics; Venkatraman Ramakrishnan (2009) in Chemistry; Kailash Satyarthi (2014) for peace and Abhijit Baerjee (2019) for Economics Sciences.

There are many Indian scientists, who may not have got the Nobel Prize but they have made a very significant contribution in raising our prestige worldwide by their inventions. Names of scientists like Homi Jehangir Bhaba (Nuclear Science); Vikram Sarabhai (space Science); Satish Dhawan (supersonic wind tunnel); APJ Abdul Kalam (missile projects); Shanti Swarup Bhatnagar (colloid Chemist); T R Seshadri, FRS (organic Chemist); S M Mukherjee, Kurukshetra University (organic chemist); B S Khandelwal, IIT, Delhi and Prof emeritus (inorganic chemistry) and thousands of scientists, engineers like Vishvesariya, the first astronaut, Rakesh Malhotra and many more have been awfully busy throughout the world in making life of their citizens more comfortable and happier.

We can remain healthy and happy by remembering the contributions of such dignitaries and narrating their inspiring stories to our children and grandchildren.

Employees and officers working in public or private sectors have a very important role to play to keep citizens by their loyalty to their companies, but working with honesty and sincerity in the interest of the Nation. Similar is the role of lawmakers of states and Federal Govt. to keep working in the interest of the country with honesty and devotion so that its people remain safe, carefree and happy. Our forces deployed on national boundaries are protecting us all from the heinous designs of our enemies. We citizens of any nation can remain happy and have a sound sleep by their untiring and 24 hours duty on our boundaries. We have always been expressing and should keep appreciating our gratitude to our forces, who always put their life in danger just to keep us safe and happy. If our forces are protecting our national boundaries, the local policemen are helping us all inside our localities and communities by providing us with the best law and order situations and saving us from local goons and antisocial elements. We may again express our gratitude and pay a very big salute to local police as well for keeping us safe and happy.

A happy mind resides in a healthy body. Thus we may remain joyful and healthy by doing excellent work in our own fields and by expressing gratitude to officials and soldiers of our forces and the para military forces.

Most of the above categories of people belong to the elite group of the society. But the common man of every country in every field never lags behind by working for their country in different ways. All of them always think of bringing happiness on the faces of their family members, their relatives and friends, community members and ultimately making all countrymen happy by their hard work, honesty and sincerity towards their duty. Doctors, nurses, paramedical staff, people working in different sectors like postal service, railways, transport and even petty shopkeepers play a very important role in bringing shine to the faces of their fellow beings. Farmers grow food grains, vegetables and beautiful flowers in their fields. We can't remain happy and satisfied without their help. Even petty workers like cobblers, fishermen, postmen, bank clerks and officials, railway men of every category, domestic helpers at our homes and offices, nearby shops, theaters, gyms, malls are a great help to us all. We appreciate their help in our daily chores from morning till late night and they make us happy. All such people around us are always busy doing jobs very sincerely, making our community members, residents of our city / council, district , state and ultimately our Nation great and spreading the fragrance of cheerfulness around us.

Whenever we work with honesty, sincerity and love for the job; keeping the country always at the first place, we keep ourselves happy and make the whole country happy. Hence, the Nation First and the Rest Next should be our motto.

A few of the following activities may help us in taking our nation ahead and to keep us happy:

1. Am I always concerned about punctuality?
2. Do I perform my task to my fullest satisfaction?
3. Am I always concerned about my peers and people around me?
4. Do I believe in charity to needy people, but never support begging?
5. Do I believe in working in a group by listening to others and not thrusting my view on my fellows?

CHAPTER- 8
CARE FOR NATURE

We start our day by having a look at the rising Sun, if we get up early in the morning to feel immense inner happiness of the beautiful orange red light beams coming towards us. We can enjoy this only in the early morning, otherwise the penetrating beams from the Sun reaching us after sometime are unbearable to our delicate eyes. Our early morning walk makes us more joyful by seeing the green plants, bushes, trees and multicolored flowers around us. The cool breeze fills our lungs with pure air as the roads are not crowded by vehicles emitting deadly poisonous gasses like carbon monoxide, oxides of nitrogen and sulfur. E - vehicles in many cities are a boon to us, where we can breathe in fresh air free from air pollutants. Water bodies at many places provide more positive energy to our mind and we start feeling healthy and happy after doing light exercises. Early morning walk is also beneficial to us by meeting and interacting with people of all ages walking, running and doing exercises. We also get motivated to join such people and try to make our day more joyful by talking to them and also joining them doing a few exercises, which keep us fit for the whole day.

Nature and natural surroundings give us so much, but how much care we are doing for nature. Are we not responsible for air pollution, water pollution, noise pollution and global warming by making our planet not worth living by our daily activities?

Scientists, engineers and astronauts of developed and developing countries are trying hard to find water and oxygen containing air to make life possible on some other planet. But are we not busy erecting concrete jungle around us by constructing many multi storey towers where we hardly find any greenery for our eyes and water bodies for our daily need? Every big tower is continuously emitting tons of carbon dioxide and many hundred thousands of kilocalories of heat from thousands of air conditioners from each tower. We are consuming hundreds of liters of water from each flat of the tower. Have we ever imagined the quantum of toilet rolls being consumed by us daily leading to cutting of millions of trees daily all over the globe? Situation is very grim and pathetic and days are not far away, when life may not be possible on our earth for our future generations. Tangential increase in automobiles of every kind is polluting our environment to a greater extent. Many new deadly diseases are making life more troublesome due to air, water and noise pollution. Situation around us is becoming more and more serious and hence the need for urgent steps to overcome these deadly happenings, which are increasing every moment around us.

The developed and developing countries are taking note of the alarming situations and passing resolutions to take care of the climate change. But it's the duty of each and every citizen of the world to come forward and help our respective city councils by taking urgent steps to save our Earth: controlling use of water, paper, electricity and saving energy by maximizing use of walking to nearby places, using stairs instead of lifts wherever possible and prioritizing public transportation.

Water use can be reduced to some extent by keeping the tap closed while brushing and shaving. Modern houses have the provision of showers for taking baths. Two minute shower is enough to clean the body and keep us fresh. Many households use buckets and mugs for taking baths. Mugs of smaller capacity may be helpful in controlling use of water. The water coming out of ROs (reverse osmosis) may be stored for cleaning of clothes, utensils and for watering the kitchen garden plants. By adopting these alternative ways, hundreds of liters of water can be saved daily by every household. We may go for adopting the latest techniques of saving and harvesting of water especially during the rainy season. To cite one example, we were living in a four storey building having 12 flats some 24 years ago. We went for water harvesting by taking rainwater from roofs direct to the ground by following the water harvesting treatment. The residents never felt a shortage of water in our building even during the scorching heat of central India, when many of our neighbors always felt a shortage of water every summer.

Harvesting and conservation of water should be adopted by all city councils by making small dams near the water catchment areas and should be mandatory for all buildings to tackle shortage of water by following water harvesting systems during rainy days.

Water is our life line. Life on earth is not possible without water. Two thirds of earth is occupied by seven Oceans inhabited by millions of aquatic animals, but water being salty, oceans' water is not fit for drinking by living beings- humans, animals, birds and plants and trees. In spite of such a great value of water, many rivers and lakes are being polluted by us, which is highly detrimental for our health. In the name of development, we are destroying the natural beauty, purity and serenity of our rivers and mountains. Effluents of many industries penetrate inside the Earth and pollute underground water making it unfit for drinking. Poor people living in nearby areas have to drink the polluted water containing many lethal chemicals and heavy metals like lead, Arsenic, antimony, Cobalt and Zinc responsible for many diseases to inhabitants. There is a dire need to make a separate channel for treatment of such poisonous effluents released by industries for safety and good health of residents of neighboring villages, towns and big cities. Yamuna river having origin in Yamunotri in Uttarakhand takes the shape of a dirty nullaha emitting foul smell when it reaches Delhi, the capital city of India.

Very serious floods in Uttarakhand state of India are eye openers to state government and central government officials. In 2021, faulty construction into fragile mountains caused glaciers to burst into rivers causing loss of property and life of thousands of residents and pilgrimages. The town of Joshimath in Uttarakhand had massive landslides in December 2022 and January 2023 (37). The Joshimath city and the adjoining areas of Uttarakhand became centers of anxiety on 10 July, 2023, when a glacier burst about 50 kilometers away from it, resulting in huge loss of life of many people and property. The glacial burst led to a rise in water level of the Yumma nullaha (watercourse) in the Niti valley. The drain was flooded with water similar to what was seen in Rishi Ganga on 7 Feb. 2021, washing away the Raini Bridge on that devastating day. Chamoli district received 232% more rainfall than normal on July 9 and 80% above normal rain on 10 July, 2021.

The above havoc was the result of continuous deforestation with connivance of politicians for construction of many hotels on sloppy mountains without caring for the natural environment. More than 1,300 people lost their lives during the landslides.

November 12, 2023 was the day of anxieties and concerns not only for people and the government of Uttarakhand, central government of India, but for the whole country during the entrapment of 41 tunnel workers under the Silkyra Bend - Barkot tunnel (38). The workers were constructing a 4.5 km tunnel through a fragile part of the Himalayas in spite of warnings by environmentalists. The collapse trapped workers behind a 197 ft. wall of debris, but fortunately all were saved by the untiring efforts of hundreds of rescuers including engineers, technicians, workers, and rat-hole miners by working around the clock for 17 days. The rat-hole miners did an exceptional job by digging 10 meters in 24 hours to reach the trapped exhausted workers, who never gave up in the enclosed tunnel facing every sort of problem and difficulty. This was the toughest of operations, with a great lesson for the government and the town and country planning agencies involved, ignoring many safety precautions. Family members of all trapped tunnel workers couldn't sleep for many nights, worrying about the safety of their family members. The scene of all 41 miners coming out, one-by-one from the special metal capsule from the collapsed side, was something unbelievable and the greatest gift of God to residents. It is rightly said, "All's Well That Ends Well".

There are dire needs of setting a balance between development and environment, especially for the protection of forests and maintenance of purity and serenity of our natural resources.

Air, which we can't see, is another important component for life. We remain alive only by breathing in fresh air. Air generally contains about 79% nitrogen gas, 20% oxygen and about 1.0% mixture of other gasses like oxides of carbon, nitrogen, sulfur and trace amounts of hydrogen sulfides. Humans, animals and birds breathe air from which we take oxygen, needed for flow of blood, which keeps us alive. Living beings, after taking oxygen from air, exhale carbon dioxide, which is absorbed by plants and trees around us. Plants emit oxygen back in the environment for all living things. Thus an ideal balance of oxygen, carbon dioxide is maintained in nature, but this balance is constantly disturbed by human activities, leading to different diseases all over the Earth. Use of air conditioners has become a must in almost all European, American, Australian, and in many developing countries like India facing extreme cold weather, where during snowfall, temperature falls below zero degree and at many places below -30°C to -40°C. The invention of air conditioners proved a boon for such countries, and use of ACs' became essential to keep people warm in chilly weather. In Asian, African and Arab countries, the situation was the other way round. If western countries were suffering from extreme cold weather, the eastern and Middle East countries would have to face high temperatures between 45-55°C during summers, which is unbearable to citizens of these countries, especially the countries infested with deserts and sand dunes and use of ACs become a must.

Optimum use of electricity, water and that of ACs can control this serious situation in eastern and western countries by teaching proper and optimum use only in case of very harsh situations in schools from the tender age of children, as they are taught the values of caring and sharing in developed and many developing countries.

An ordinary typical domestic AC releases from 0.625 - 1.0 pound (453 g) of CO_2 (39) in one hour and emits heat in the atmosphere resulting in global warming. Where will the emitted CO_2 and heat go? Obviously, this will go in the atmosphere. We can just imagine the magnanimity of heat caused by billions of high capacity air conditioners used throughout the globe to keep our homes, garages, parking lots, cars and offices warm in winters and cool in summers. Some 50 years back, when I started teaching in a PG college of Panjab university, we had only one fan in our family of 15 people living together. Later people started using water coolers, which didn't release much heat in the atmosphere, but kept the rooms very cool. After joining the PG college of NCERT at Bhopal in 1975, I found one air conditioner in the principal's chamber and another in the staff council room.

During our first visit to the U.S. in 1990, we found use of air conditioners everywhere starting from homes, garages, cars, offices and shopping centers. These were the luxuries for us in America but essentials for Americans to keep their lives comfortable and more so because they could afford it. Same was the situation in other countries like Great Britain, Australia, UAE, and Europe during our more visits to these countries. India and other countries of Asia, Africa and Arab countries are also not lagging behind in the name of development by constructing hundreds of multi storey towers, big malls and modern corporate offices.

We all are responsible for global warming of the Earth and for the terrible future of our coming generations, who will have to starve due to deficiency of food, water and air of any kind, if available to them.

Increase of automobiles is another menace for the existence of life on the Earth. During our first visit to America, we were amazed and astonished to see at least two cars in every small family. With the passage of time, the number of cars in every family has increased tremendously not only in developed countries but even in developing countries of all the continents leading to air and noise pollution. Greenhouse gasses are emitted by vehicles using petrol or diesel responsible for global warming. As per one estimate in 2023, a typical passenger vehicle emits about 4.6 metric tons of CO_2 (40) per year. This number can vary based on a vehicle's fuel, fuel economy, and the number of miles driven. Humpty dumpty roads are replaced tangentially in every country by well carpeted six lanes or twelve lanes roads using millions of tons of iron roads, cement, sand and gravels after cutting around 42M of trees worldwide daily (41). Humans have already destroyed around 46% of the trees on Earth. Only 36% of the world's rainforests remain intact. Three trillion trees are said to remain on our planet with a large deforestation every year. As per the above estimate, deforestation is leading to more and more global warming, causing floods, air pollution due to absence of absorption of CO_2 and particulate matter resulting from burning of fossil fuels and development of infrastructure and high towers everywhere. Glaciers are melting and sea level is increasing, predicting drowning of many low lying countries in swelling seas, which are crossing their boundaries. Over usage of water is responsible for scarcity in rivers, lakes, ponds as well as under the Earth. What to do then? We all will have to introspect very honestly without any bias. We all are responsible for erosion of soil, scarcity of water, and noise and air pollution around us.

The modern developments are root causes for making our life miserable, unhealthy and stressful. Then what to do for people all over our planet to lead a joyful and healthy life? This requires a sense of urgency by all of us besides the global and national authorities, city councils and

all communities by having micro planning at the grass root level.

Can we all think of planting 5-6 trees around our home if living in independent houses or having 15-20 flower pots or dwarf trees if living in big towers. Many communities living in enclosed campuses are found to have a few parks with lush green lawns and varieties of trees including a few medicinal trees to keep us healthy. Many households are found to develop kitchen gardens in the back yards. In western countries, each household has a beautiful front yard with lush green grassy lawns embedded with multicolored flowers and backyards with a few fruit trees and space for family kids to play. If farmers of northern India grow different types of crops and varieties of fruits and flowers, every household of South India has provision of a few coconut trees in the front yard and the backyard with multicolored flowers and a few medicinal plants of daily use. By doing so, household owners tend to remain very close to nature and they remain healthy and happy.

Let's plant a few flowering, medicinal or shady trees at our home or in our neighborhood for absorption of CO2 exhaled by us and automobiles to keep a good balance of fresh air in the atmosphere to contribute in reducing global warming and remain joyful and healthy.

Ours will be a great contribution in saving earth by saving water with optimum use, and harvesting it during the rainy season in various ways adopted by local people as our forefathers used to follow during their lifetimes. Water Bawdies (reservoirs or big water wells) are very common in Rajasthan (42) in India which about 1-2 centuries ago used to be the desert with scarcity of rains and almost every house owner made the provision of such Bawdies in their small or big homes. Roof harvesting system of Mandu fort (43) is exemplary for storing rain water for months for residents of the fort in case of attack by the enemy. Next may be periodic cleaning of wells / Bawdies, not washing clothes in nearby dams or rivers, which are very common in many Asian countries, where people take baths in the open. This will be a useful step to check water pollution of nearby wells, dams and rivers. A few religious events and taboos are prevailing in societies of different religions, which they follow by throwing flowers and other items after worship in rivers or wells without knowing that we are inviting water pollution again. Most of us throw sacred items after worship at home or in temples or mosques in sacred water of rivers without thinking that vegetables, flowers etc. will stagnate after coming in contact with water leading to water pollution and giving a foul smell. There is a dire need to educate people, who pollute wells, rivers or dams unknowingly without understanding the after effects of their activity.

Let's conserve and harvest, save water by using it judiciously and avoid throwing flowers etc. in nearby wells, rivers or dams to keep our water resources clean. Polluted water is responsible for many diseases. This is our pious duty to keep water resources very neat and clean and free from pollutants to lead a healthy and happy life.

What do we think of the ever increasing number of vehicles and their over usage? How many cars and automobiles do we have in each household? How many of us really care for car pooling for going to offices or for some common parties/get-together/excursions to save fuel and minimize air and noise pollution? The overuse of cars can be controlled by going to the office by carpooling. Three or four people can use one car by rotation. All of us will remain healthy and happy and help the community and the nation in many ways. By doing so, besides controlling air and noise pollution and saving fuel, this will help in developing better bonding between office goers by adopting carpooling and also a step in controlling our monthly budget.

Electricity is one of the very important parameters to bring happiness in our life for our comforts by using different appliances invented by our creative scientists and engineers 2-3 centuries ago, but overuse of electricity has been widely responsible for the main problem of global warming. Most of the developing countries are generating electricity by thermal power stations, though switching lately to alternative means like wind energy, tidal energy, solar energy and pollution-free nuclear energy. This Should be remembered by advocates of nuclear energy plants that very strict precautions during construction of nuclear power plants are observed. The quantum of electricity used by developed countries is much higher than the requirement of developing countries. To cite one simple example, 86.36M of households of the U. S. out of 127M households (68%) use dishwashers for cleaning of utensils. By using one dishwasher of 1800

Watt model for one hour, 1.8 kWh of electricity (44) is used. Thus, 86.36M households of America use 155.45M kWh of electricity per day (assuming only one usage for one hour). Coming to India, less than one percent of households out of 324M (45) use dishwashers and they require only 5.83M kWh of electricity. We can thus conclude that American households using dishwashers for one hour daily are found to consume 26.67 times more electricity than Indian households only by using one electrical appliance and partly responsible for global warming.

There are many more such examples of global warming by developed countries and harming our Earth and natural habitations around us. This is one of the causes of poor health and unhappiness. It will be in the fitness of things to make use of every sort of energy very judiciously to save our nature for our good health and happiness.

Some of us might have heard about the use of bicycles by many politicians of different countries. Bicycles are the best way of saving fuel and help in controlling air and noise pollution. Bicycle use is becoming very common with many other benefits too. Bicycle riding helps us in making our muscles strong. Cycling also helps us in keeping our lungs healthy by consuming more oxygen. Students use cycles as the cost free mode of movement in universities these days, where departments are situated away from their hostels. A large number of students of almost all IITs, IIMs and doctors of big hospitals like AIIMs and other big hospitals of India and foreign universities use bicycles. For 4-5 km, cycle use is very helpful for bringing groceries or vegetables from the market. In many countries, we have seen many cars with 2-3 bicycles at the back of their cars while going for picnics or some excursions, where parents and their kids enjoy cycle rides under the open sky.

Let's help our community, city council and the nation in controlling air and noise pollution, plant thousands of trees in one stroke to reduce deforestation and reduce the over usage of water, electricity and cars by carpooling and cycling for short distances to keep us joyful and healthy.

Some of the following activities, if followed by us at our homes and offices can save a lot of water and electricity to reduce our bills.

1. We can save a large quantity of water by closing taps and using small mugs while shaving and brushing teeth.

2. If we sit in one room for family Get- Together, we can save a lot of energy by switching off fans and tube lights in other rooms.

3. We can increase our happiness by planting a few dwarf trees and flowery plants in our front yards and backyards. Planting 2 medicinal plants will keep us healthy and happy.

4. We can control global warming by walking 10,000 steps daily, using stairs in four storey buildings and making use of bicycles for short distances

CHAPTER – 9
LATEST INVENTIONS & MODERN FAMILY LIFE

There is one very meaningful old saying that man is a social animal. All of us will surely agree that we get immense internal happiness when we greet our colleagues in the office in the morning. When we teachers enter the class, our first sentence is, "Good morning dear boys and girls. How are you"? Most of the doctors in developed countries and now in many developing countries also welcome their patients at the entry point and ask them to take a seat. Such a gesture of a doctor helps in relieving pain of the patient to some extent and the patient feels at home to discuss the problem with ease in a relaxed way. We greet our sweet heart and lovely kids and hug them after reaching home in the evening and our all tiredness or anxieties of the whole day fades away within a few seconds, making us all very cheerful. No less happy moments are those when our parents, grandparents, some relatives or some old friends visit us after a long time as they are very selflessly and deeply attached with us. Their visits make us happy internally and externally as well.

Sometime back, we were living in a joint family system enjoying very strong bonding with all family members. Besides parents, many brothers and sisters, grandparents and sometimes great-grandparents also were a part of the big family a few years ago. All family members listened to their advice with great reverence and each member enjoyed the happiness or sorrows of the family as one entity. The elderly members had their children and grandchildren at their beck and call and the younger ones always felt safe and secure under the mentorship of their parents and grandparents.

There were only a very few means of transportation and communication and only a few ways of entertainment some 50-60 years ago. Movements of the family members were limited to their adjoining fields or nearby workplace. All members enjoyed family togetherness over lunch or dinner in one room, where all were free to discuss their day to day problems, with immediate solutions by the elderly members based upon their life experiences. There used to be a very close knit relationship between all with respect to parents and grandparents and love for children and grandchildren. Story telling or listening to life experiences from their elders were the real past times after dinner in the night, making family bonds stronger and stronger every day. The young kids waited for the interesting stories or anecdotes for the next day. All members were in the habit of getting up early in the morning and listening to religious songs from their mother/grandmother besides inculcation of life values in all the family members. Daily bath with cold water was a dictum for all, followed by family prayers before going to school or work. This was the life pattern of any ordinary middle class Indian family some 70 years ago, as observed by many of us. During my childhood and even after becoming a professor, we 15 family members used to live in two small rooms, but we were always the happiest lot due to the shadow of our loving parents on our heads and by the grace of God as well. The same may be true with households of other South Asian countries.

But the above pattern is rarely observed these days in most families with a few exceptions due to development and modernization taking place all over the world at a very rapid pace. As stated earlier, people are shifting to nearby towns, cities and other states or even to developed countries for higher education. Even and girls don't hesitate to move to other states for higher education and even to other countries in search of jobs or vertical mobility in their career. The world has become very small due to very fast means of transportation and communication. East and West, North and South are not far away for awfully busy business persons, big corporations and politicians these days. Starting from Japan in the East, meeting family members in Sydney, Newcastle, San Francisco, and London; presenting a research paper in some international conference in cosmopolitan cities of India, one can reach the home town within a week. This is possible by fast means of transportation achieved by the untiring efforts of scientists, engineers, technicians and managers of big companies all over the world. But high dreams of individuals like Steven Jobs, Elon Musk, Bill Gates, Mark Zukerberg, Sunder Pitchai, Satya Nadela, Arvind Krishnan of IBM and hundreds of other innovators have changed the scenario of the world during the last 70 years.

By his constant persistence, devotion, dedication and imagination in spite of opposition of his co-workers, Steve Jobs (12) succeeded in introducing the world with the cordless iPhone and iPad (during his Interim Chairmanship of Apple company) as mentioned earlier after making different models of Apple computers. Engineers, scientists and thousands of employees at Apple have been constantly busy in developing newer and newer models of iPhones, sleek laptops, and ipads with many new configurations even after the death of Steve Jobs. Though Steve raised his company to a billionaire company, but, whatever his company earned, he invested back in the company. Though an owner of the billion dollar company, Steve took only one dollar per annum as his salary. Steve Job's imagination of cordless phones in spite of tough opposition by his teammates changed the scenario of the world by bringing us very close to each other by his persistence and continuous and long lasting efforts. Steve Jobs' team members loved him a lot, valued his imagination in spite of differences with him during his leadership and kept working on his ideas even after Steve's death with active support of young scientists, engineers, technicians and innovators working in other companies by invention of smartphones.

Steve Jobs's last words from his deathbed are worth reading and following in life, which are exemplary for all of us in today's materialistic world, when Jobs emphasizes the value and importance of family and friends in life.

The contribution of William Henry Gates, popularly known as Bill Gate (46), an American businessman owning Microsoft with the current value of more than 133 billion dollars is another example worth mentioning. Bill co-founded Microsoft Corporation in 1975 with Paul Allen and led the company to become the worldwide leader in business and software services.

William Henry Gate will be remembered as owner of Microsoft, as a philanthropist, as an investor and as a writer for many years to come.

Mark Elliot Zuckerberg, a young American technocrat born on 14 May, 1984 (47) invented the Facebook platform for bringing the whole world very close to each other. Most of us share our pictures, happenings of our family or official events and celebrations with our friends, family members or relatives living at faraway places. It is rightly said by our ancestors that happiness increases by sharing with family, friends and relatives, whereas painful events reduce our grief and sorrows by sharing.

Mark Zuckerberg's worth of 176 billion U.S. dollars makes him the 4th richest person, but his innovations extended far beyond in new areas of connectivity initiatives, AI (Artificial Intelligence), virtual reality, philanthropy, and the metaverse shaping the technological world and defining the future of digital interaction.

Smart phones have become very common from which we can get any information within a few seconds. Google, Gemini, and Sirie have increased our learning many folds, fastening our way of living and keeping us up to date and happy. Even people living in slums, remote rural areas, domestic helpers and petty workers possess smartphones and their level of learning is increasing by enhancement of literacy of people. IT is also playing an immense role in our life. Sitting at home, we can get our travel tickets booked. We can send our research papers to journals for publication in any part of the world in no time. We can find the position of flights, trains and the location of our wards sitting at home. We can watch many entertaining programs during travel to avoid our boredom and get refreshed. Everyone can't go to the Olympic city to watch games, but we can watch many events sitting in our drawing room with much comfort, thousands of kilometers away from the Olympic village. Worldwide business has become very fast and very easy with the invention of smartphones.

Online classes proved a great boon to students sitting at their homes during Covid - 19 pandemic in 2020 and 2022. Employees enjoyed the facility of working from homes by grace of corporate offices of MNCs. The companies also benefited by saving office rents, water and electricity bills by allowing their staff to work from home. But some negative effects were also observed due to constant sitting at home. Some intelligent people continued exercises at home and continued walking on roads of their campus but many became lethargic and increased their weight.

Mothers invented a unique way of keeping their 3-4 month babies busy by showing them cartoons or rhymes by keeping an iPhone close to their tummy, while working in the kitchen or working from home without being disturbed by crying kids. Overuse of smartphones is increasing day by day. Excess of screen time is disturbing our lifestyle besides affecting our eyes and spoiling our health. Children, youth and people of all ages develop many physical and mental problems. If smartphones are a boon to us to make our lives more entertaining, comfortable and bring us very close to the world, making us up to date and increasing our knowledge, and to remain happy. But overuse of the same is spoiling our health, as most of us now are not devoting time to regular exercises leading to numerous health issues.

New inventions surely make our lives more comfortable, happy and convenient, but judicious and meticulous use of new gadgets may help us in keeping a good balance between comforts, our health and social settings in our life..

The latest development is the flooding of electric vehicles, especially by the arrival of Tesla by Elon Musk (48). By the end of 2022, Tesla had delivered 405,300 electric vehicles in the U.S. alone. Globally, Tesla delivered over 1.3M EVs, but the history of electric vehicles dates back to 1830 when inventors in Europe and America began experimenting with battery power and electric car designs in their companies. The first crude electric vehicle was developed by Scottish inventor Robert Anderson around 1832 (49). German engineer Andreas Flocken built the first electric car in 1888. The first electric bus was made by Scania-Vabis T-31 in 1940 (50) and the company delivered 120 bus chassis from 1940 to

1951 to Stockholm's public transport company. These trolley buses were produced in partnership with the electric company ASEA and Swedish bodybuilder Hagglund and Soner.

E-buses are becoming very common in India and many other countries. We enjoyed our Europe trip with our 13-years-old grandson Kunal to Germany, Switzerland, Italy and France by traveling thousands of kilometers by traveling in air conditioned E-buses without facing any noise and air pollution. E-buses were recently introduced on many routes in India a few years ago. We use the E-bus while visiting Kavita and her children living in Indore. These buses are air conditioned and run by lithium batteries and don't cause any pollution. They take less time and seats are booked in advance with the phone from our home.

Our genesis is from a small village of Sonipat district of India, where we lived together under one roof some 70 years ago before shifting to the nearby town, Sonipat. Though our family members live now at faraway places, we remain connected with each other with the help of smartphones to know the welfare of each family member. We visit family members on joyful events and painful moments of life. Whenever we meet our growing children and grandchildren, we always have the feeling of joy, positive energy and a great sense of satisfaction to learn about their progress. Each brother and sister owns beautiful houses in their respective cities. Their children are doing extremely well at their workplace or their own companies. With our genesis from a small village, our big family has 8 doctors, 12 engineers, 7 bankers, 10 teachers including two university professors with Ph. D degree, and more than 5 members running their own business in different fields by grace of God and our visionary father, who educated all of us to the university level. Every family member feels proud to be a member of such an enlightened family serving our own country and giving services in foreign countries as well, making almost every member very happy and healthy and also making people around them happy.

After my superannuation as professor of chemistry from NCERT, the national level body of government of India in 2007, we made Bhopal, capital of India as our permanent home. Our eldest son Bobby Gupta left for Australia in 1999 to join a multinational company in Sydney after doing MBA from Queensland University of Technology (QUT) of Brisbane, and serving in India for some time. Bobby kept inviting us to have quality time with Kunal, our 6 years old grandson. We tried to inculcate a scientific attitude in the growing lad by performing a simple activity of a burning candle and writing his observations. Kunal loved playing with magnetic toys and used to think of the reason for attraction and repulsion between two ends of the bar magnet. At Diwali time, while doing Laxmi pooja, whatever we wrote in our family diary and reading out to my wife Usha, Bobby and Shuchita, Kunal kept writing on the tissue paper kept near us. Thus Kunal started inculcating critical observation skills from the very beginning. We used to get inner happiness by sitting with a 6-year-old kid during our stay. We recall those days with great fondness, when we used to visit different sea beaches and find Kunal busy making a tomb with sand.

Visit to family members while in service and even after superannuation, keep strengthening of childhood bonds with children and grandchildren to remain healthy and happy. Moreover, when we visit our children and grandchildren they start taking care of us, making both parents and grandparents very happy and satisfied. New inventions have made our life more convenient and comfortable. It is up to us how to keep a balance between facilities and family life.

The following activities may help us in keeping good relations with family members:

1. Never push our opinion on others as everyone has a brain and different way of thinking.

2. Sacrifice is the greatest tool to win the hearts of family members.

3. Always remaining truthful is the gurumantra of success of a happy family, since truth lasts long and wins the hearts of everyone.

4. Remain straight forward, but listen to all. Listening to others develops confidence in us.

5. Must visit family members in distress to share their sorrows, as visiting them on happy occasions.

CHAPTER -10
FAMILY MEMBERS

Bobby and Shuchita were working in IBM and leading a very happy life in Australia. We visited the capital city, Canberra to meet Bobby, Shuchita, Kunal and Aryan wherefrom we planned to visit the Gold Coast by road. It was very thrilling to drive for 1100 kilometers in our car from Canberra to Gold Coast. After reaching the shining city of Gold Coast, we found thousands of surfers in the sea with their surfing boards. It was a very neat and clean ambience with surfers of different countries enjoying the waves with the rise and fall of the tide. We also got a chance to visit QUT (Queensland University of Technology), Bobby's alma mater from where he completed his MBA in 1997. Visiting different countries helps us a lot to visit important cities, understand the culture of the people of those countries, but family values are observed as the common factor everywhere. Meeting people from other countries is a great source of learning about their way of living, their culture and happiness.

We had been to Sydney earlier and were lucky enough to visit Darling Harbor situated on the shore of the Pacific Ocean. Darling Harbor is so beautiful with its positive vibes of its surroundings and the hustle and bustle of thousands of tourists till midnight. The Sydney Harbor is one of the largest natural harbors of the world, which is believed to have been an estuary with bays and inlets that was drowned during a flood brought on by a sudden rise in the sea level some 17,00 years ago (51). The harbor was redeveped by announcement of plans by the then Premier Mr. Neville Wran in 1984 and opened to the public by Queen Elizabeth on May 4, 1988 (52).

The Opera House (53), situated on the Darling Harbor, is the cultural hub where artists of Australia and many other nationalities perform their singing, dancing and other cultural activities. The Opera House was constructed in four stages from 1957-1973. The Sydney Opera House is an Australian icon for performers of multipurpose arts and a symbol of Sydney and Australia around the world. It has a 2679 - seat concert hall, opened to the public in 1973, where again we found thousands of visitors of different ages, and of different nationalities thronging there. We could also visit the world famous Australian Harbor Arch Bridge (54), connecting the northern and southern shores of Sydney Harbor. It is one of the longest steel-arch bridges in the world. Along its length, it features four railroad tracks, a highway, and two pedestrian walkways, avoiding traffic congestion to a very great extent. Total length of the bridge is 1,149 meters (3770 ft). Many tourists dare to have a strenuous walk on Harbor Bridge to test their stamina. The Harbor steel-arch Bridge acts as a machine to test the strength of tourists. Vineet and Deepika with many tourists from different countries succeeded in completing the walk on the bridge in two hours.

When Bobby and Shuchita got their new assignments in Dubai after their promotions, we had the luxury of visiting the UAE with its many world record sights - namely largest Dubai Mall, tallest Burj Khalifa, Burj Al Arab hotel with provision of helicopter landing and the largest Hotel Atlantis and many multi-story residential towers. Law and order of Dubai is worth praising. Ladies are very safe and they can be seen walking on roads till late night. Dubai and Abu Dhabi are the most sought destinations for tourists from all over the world as UAE is a very popular shopping destination due to being a tax free country. Being situated on the shore of Arabian Sea, hotel Atlantis and Burj Al Arab have been raised by filling the sea. Most of the developments in Dubai and Abu Dhabi have taken place during the last 25 years due to the vision of the President and Prime Minister of UAE with a firm message to the concerned agencies to complete all projects within the set time limit.

UAE is surrounded by deserts with no potable water, but the President and Prime Minister of the country have changed the desert into the most favorite tourist country by desalination of seawater making it fit for drinking. Rains are very rare but every drop of water is saved by using water with sprinklers, and tourists are pleased to see greenery near hotels and restaurants. It's always a pleasure to have a walk on JBR (Jumeirah Beach Residence) and many other places with shops of European style architecture on one side of the road and Arabian Sea on the other side. Cleaners start cleaning the roads early in the morning to make them dust and sand free. Dubai and Abu Dhabi are the cities worth visiting with family and relatives to gain more positive energy in a country very close to India with 80 percent Indians running business with their partners in UAE.

We visited America for the first time with Usha, her younger sister Sarita and her husband MKG (Mahender Kumar Gupta). After shifting Bobby, Shuchita, Kunal and Aryan in 2013 from Dubai to California, we again got chances to revisit America in 2015, 2017, 2021 and 2024. Bobby is running his own company as an advisor to many global companies in America, Australia, Canada and India, and a venture capitalist and founder of AI companies. Shuchita is global CTO of a multinational company and is always in much demand due to her super knowledge in computers and IT. I have had very old associations with world famous Stanford University since 1976, when I undertook a national project in my college of NCERT on Microteaching - Teacher Training Project conceived and developed by professors of Stanford University. We got a chance to visit Stanford University 2-3 times with Bobby and Naren.

Entry to the university crossing over the multicolored flower beds and lush green lawns fill visitors with positive energy. It's always a great pleasure to visit Stanford University, which motivates young and even elderly persons to be students of such a top class university.

During our visit to America in 2017, we were thrilled for Kunal, getting admission in UCB (University of California, Berkeley). We were amazed to locate an exclusive parking lot for seven Nobel Laureates in front of the Astro Physics Department, meaning thereby that seven Nobel Laureates were still in the faculty of UCB and they may work all the seven days both during the day and the night. Both Stanford and UC have the credit of having many Professors, who are honored with the most prestigious Nobel Awards. Such achievements of dedicated faculty members are great inspirations for teachers all over the world.

We could have a chance to visit beautiful sea beaches, lighthouses, redwood forests, and the Golden Gate of San Francisco. Walking on the bridge with showers of cool bridges always fills the visitors with utmost freshness. Many people living in San Francisco have the luxury of walking on the Golden Gate Bridge in the morning or evening to fill their lungs with pure air to increase their longevity. We were doubly benefitted by our visit to the U.S.A. in 2024 to learn that Aryan got admission in UCB justifying the old saying, "Like Elders, Like Younger". Kunal gave us the good news about joining a startup as a founder engineer for harnessing AI as an education tool for universities.

Both Kunal and Aryan always keep us in good humor; healthy and happy. We are always filled with joy and extreme happiness to visit them and receive their phone calls regularly from the U.S.

Kavita owns a house in Bhopal and after working for about 20 years in Bhopal, she relocated to Indore which is about 200 kilometers from Bhopal. Kavita has been working as a laparoscopic surgeon in Bombay Hospital, Indore for the last five years and has earned a name as an outstanding surgeon in Indore. Kavita is a prominent member of many societies of Indore, M.P. and India and has participated in many national and international conferences. Kavita's elder daughter Yashasvi is serving in some multinational company after doing BS from IIT Delhi. Yashasvi brought honor to the family by earning NTS Scholarship from NCERT and IISc. Bangalore. Yashasvi also represented India as a member of different countries at the Australian Science Olympiad, Sydney. Aayush is studying in year 12 in a renowned school of Indore and honored as a Headboy of the school for the session 2024-2025. Aayush is trying to be a web designer and animator. He is a much sought designer in central India and won many awards in making small films. We both keep visiting Indore quite often.

Kavita and her children always take us to nearby tourists' destinations enhancing our joy. Indore has the honor of getting the Award of cleanest city of India for the sixth time in a row. It's always a great pleasure to visit a very neat and clean city, also known for its delicious food and to visit many temples of Indore and Ujjain. Visiting Mahakal at Ujjain is always a rewarding day and so is the case of visiting Khajrana temple of Lord Ganesh, Pitra Pravat of Lord Hanuman and Devi Ahilya temple in Rajwada. There are many other tourists' spots, especially 56 food shops, where every tourist wants to go to enjoy varieties of delicacies. There are many nearby resorts worth visiting to increase our knowledge, enjoy different kinds of food items, positive energy by meditation in open lawns and freshness emanating from greenery all around.

Our visits to Australia have multiplied after the settling of Deepika at Newcastle after working for two years at the West Mead hospital in Sydney from 2005 – 2007. Deepika is a pediatrician and is now a super specialist in her field. Deepika earned a very good name while working as a senior specialist at John Hunter Hospital for about more than 10 years. Dr. Deepika is a much sought doctor by children having abuse of any kind and parents as their caretakers from far and flung areas of New South Wales prefer to visit Deepika for counseling of their children, which imparts a soothing effect to them and their parents as well. A few years back, Deepika opened "Ishana Well-Being Center" for the benefit of the community of Newcastle. One hall is kept exclusively for persons doing meditation, which makes the center extraordinary in the sense that it is open for everyone without any cost. Deepika is Director of the Center. Ishana Well-Being Center, in true sense, is the source of happiness and good health for the community of Newcastle and the adjoining areas of NSW (New South Wales). The center has 3-4 doctors of other fields including a psychiatrist rendering their services to the incoming patients. Ishana Well- Being Center helps John Hunter Hospital by guiding their doctors during their registrar ship period. The center has one manager and 3-4 nursing staff, who are very meticulous in their jobs bringing good fame and name to the center. Deepika is quite popular among her fraternity, nursing staff and the community by her social and helping attitude for everyone irrespective of caste, creed, and nationality. Deepika has been nominated as one of the leading businessperson, and all alone from the doctors' fraternity. A matter of great happiness and pleasure for all family members.

Vineet has been running Edgeworth Family Practice at Newcastle for the last 15 years. The practice is very close to Ishana Well- Being Center and Vineet has made his name by his excellent bonding with his old and new patients. Vineet's Family Practice is one of the topmost 1 percent G.Ps of Newcastle rendering highly commendable service to the community.

Vineet and Deepika are running their practices to their best and fullest satisfaction of their patients and nursing staff, treating them as family members, which always keeps them healthy, happy and loyal to their clinics.

Vineet has been practicing Karate and has earned Black Belt this year. Vineet is fond of singing and no Newcastle party is complete without his melodious song. Deepika is a renowned dancer and also started learning singing. They have two children- Anshul and Ishana. Both are doing extremely well in academics, besides participating in many extra- curricular activities like music, debates, and quiz competitions. Vineet, Anshul and Ishana are regular visitors to Karate class. Anshul got the Black Belt this year. Both Vineet and Anshul earned 1st Dan Black Belts directly from Japan in the 1st week of July, 2024. Both Anshul and Ishana keep earning many awards from their school and in inter- school competitions every year. We both keep visiting them after every 2-3 years and are glad to see them having very good bonding with fellow Indians. They are regular visitors to Vedic Hindu temples and render service for the temple and the visitors. We also ensure to visit the Hindu Temple and feel extremely happy to meet their fellow Indian friends.

Newcastle Lake is our favorite destination whenever we visit Newcastle. Serenity, purity of lake water, young boys and girls sitting on benches, children playing in the ground and a shopping center on one side of the lake makes it a favorable meeting place for people of all ages. White ducks on the shore of the lake are an attraction for everyone. Some children are found engaged in throwing small pebbles in the lake making troughs and crests over the water. Our joy knew no bounds to find the well equipped barbecues on the shore of the lake with water and gas facility for locals to enjoy a picnic on weekends. There are washrooms with facilities of water, liquid soap and tissue papers, something unbelievable in parks of India and many other countries. Whenever we visit Newcastle, Deepika and Vineet make sure to take us to Sydney to say our "hello" to the beautiful Darling Harbor, Opera House and Harbor Bridge in Sydney. Visit to the sea world followed by a pizza party with Anshul and Ishana during that visit made our day. Food at Zafran is always an unforgettable spot of Sydney to fill us with joy for full satisfaction of our tummy and happiness of mind and brain. Visit to such places opens our horizons in new natural settings on land and ocean.

Our children and grandchildren are doing well and taking our legacy ahead. They are doing exceedingly well at their respective workplaces and schools, having a balanced life with games, sports, singing and dancing. They also keep

themselves engaged in philanthropic work for noble causes, helping the needy and downtrodden, doing social service, and also engaging with the community, which makes them all very lovable citizens bubbling with enthusiasm, good health and cheerfulness.

Whenever we leave for America or Australia, we always ensure to visit our parents (when they are alive), elder and younger brothers to take blessings of elders and good wishes of our younger ones. It is customary in our culture to touch the feet of elders, while going out of the home to another city or country for official or social gathering. Many of us bow down before our deities in Temples, Mosques, Churches and Gurdwaras to take blessings of the same God.

We are of the firm belief that bowing down before God, elders of the family or the elderly community members bestows upon us their blessings and best wishes for our good health, comfortable journey, success in our work with joy and prosperity. This custom we have been following for the last 50 years.

Ours is a very big family and happiness and sorrows are two sides of the coin. Good events are well decided beforehand, but sufferings come all of a sudden and without any notice. On every such occasion we used to visit our family in Sonipat, where our roots lie, which are now shifted to nearby Delhi and NOIDA. When we had school going children, they always waited for summer vacations to be with their uncles, aunts, cousins and grandparents. Those days used to be the days for better bonding with family members.

Loving and caring for one another, playing together, eating together, sharing our school experiences and sometimes getting angry over trivial issues, and then approaching their grandfather or older uncle to settle their scores. Our roof was the assembly point after dinner. At night, all members of the family would listen to the hours-long stories by our father and then go to sleep in different parts of the house. Time passed without a flicker of eyes, each family member felt a rejuvenation of mind, soul and body. This was the summation theory, which kept all family members healthy and happy.

One aspect that may seem very strange to the readers is that we used to share our clothes, belongings and even money with each other. Nothing was personal. Everything belonged to everyone. We, brothers, children, nephews and nieces, used to take dinner together, sometimes all sharing from one big plate sitting together on the floor.

One glass of hot milk for every member was a must before going to bed. The above activities of all family members kept us all healthy and happy and a carefree family under the patronage of our parents.

Another interesting custom of our family is an old tradition that still carries on to this day. Before going to bed, we used to press the legs of our father and give a simple massage to him during or after listening to an interesting story from him. This tradition has percolated to the lower level to our brothers and nephews. Whenever we visit our brothers stationed at different places, our younger brothers and all family members bow down before us and the younger brother starts pressing our legs in the night to give more comfort to our body. Our son always presses the legs of both of us without fail in spite of our reluctance but he never listens and keeps giving us more and more comfort. Same values are instilled in our grandchildren. All of them pay us great regards, take care of our needs and serve us during the day or night. They are very caring and sharing, even after becoming adults or on the verge of reaching adulthood.

It is observed that whenever we pay respect to others and bow down before our elders, we are sure to get their blessings and best wishes, which plays a crucial role in keeping us healthy and happy. We are sure to march on the path of success with a carefree mind. Let's give up our ego, inculcate the value of forgiving and forgetting to enjoy the beauty of life.

CHAPTER-11
RELATIVES, FRIENDS & OTHERS

Visits to relatives used to be very frequent and quite common sometime back, but in the fast world of today, people are busy with their own affairs and rarely find time for relatives, friends and family. We have forgotten to share our sorrows and sufferings as we have neither bosom friends nor selfless relatives. Most of us become victims of negative thoughts and undergo depression. Young boys and girls become prey to this disease in the more and more competitive world. Number of jobs as per our qualifications may be only a few thousands, but there are millions of aspirants even for petty jobs. How can everyone get admission into top-class medical and engineering colleges? The result is depression due to an adolescent child being scared of parents and can't express their anxieties to anyone, leading to unwanted happenings around us. So there is always a need to visit elderly members of the family, relatives or friends for solace abd and their valuable guidance.

There are some interesting and praiseworthy traditions of foreign countries. Most of the boys and girls after attaining the age of 16, try to settle in life after staying with friends. Parents also wish to make them independent. However, they keep meeting their parents off and on. One very interesting aspect is the celebration of Mother's Day and Father's Day. Sons and daughters visit their parents without fail on these days by traveling even thousands of kilometers and the most amusing celebration of "A Great Family Get-Together". An exemplary American custom is Thanksgiving, celebrated throughout America on the last Thursday of November. People take leave for Friday and thus get four days for the celebration. A majority of Americans visit their parents/friends for Thanksgiving each year. This is the best example of meeting parents, brothers, sisters and friends. This is their way of getting happiness by meeting family members at least once in a year, whether living far away or in nearby areas.

Thanksgiving is an exemplary celebration of Americans, where all family members meet their parents, brothers, sisters and friends to express their gratitude towards them. They get together over lunch or dinner and recall their old days spent together. We may follow such a beautiful celebration if we like and start celebrating in our own way.

During my 50 years of teaching career, thousands of students have passed through my different colleges of Panjab University, NCERT and engineering colleges, which have become universities of repute now. Many of them remain in touch. We also meet a few during Alumni meets. A few of them are in constant touch with our family to know our welfare and some of them come from their homes in distant places to pay their regards to us. One of such students is Jasbir Kaur, who did B.Sc. B.Ed from our teacher training college at Bhopal, a constituent unit of NCERT. I was her teacher for three years from 1975-78. She was awarded "Dr. Shankar Dayal Sharma Gold Medal" for achieving excellence in her academics and extracurricular activities during her four years course. Based upon her merit, she got the job of a science teacher in KVS (Kendriya Vidyalaya Sangathan) in Govt. of India and was posted at Central school, Bhopal. After getting a job as a science teacher, she took admission in M.Sc. Chemistry in a P.G. She used to come to our home on the college campus over the weekends for guidance and to clarify doubts about some topics. She developed a very good bond with Usha. She got a promotion after completing M.Sc. and was promoted as P.G.T. (Post Graduate Teacher). Our son and elder daughter got a chance to be her students at Bhopal school. Jasbir Kaur enjoyed the reputation of an excellent teacher of her organization. Jasbir got married to a renowned scientist of Panjab University Chandigarh, one of the best towns of India and we have been in constant touch for the last 48 years increasing our happiness in old age.

Chandigarh, the dream city of the first Prime Minister of India, Pandit Jawahar Lal Nehru, was planned by the famous French architect Le Corbusier (55). Jasbir lives very close to Chandigarh in Manali. Jasbir kept insisting us to visit their home at Manali sometime. Surendra Gupta, cousin of Usaha settled with his wife, son and daughter-in-law at Panchkula, closeby town of Manali after his retirement from Reserve Bank of India, New Delhi. We had not visited them in a long time. So we made a program to visit Surendra and Jasbir at Panchkula and Manali in 2018. Meeting them after so many years proved highly rewarding and we got new positive energy after meeting

Surendra, his wife and lovely son and daughter-in-law. They took us to the famous rose garden and Chandigarh Lake, which I had earlier visited in 1971 during COSIP (College Science Improvement Program) of the govt. of India at the Chemistry department of Panjab University. Next day we visited Jasbir and enjoyed a delicious lunch with her and her husband, a very intelligent Professor and scientist of Panjab University.

My two students, Dr. L.N. Pandey and Amod Sharma, live at Rewa, the district town of Madhya Pradesh (M.P.). Dr. Pandey completed his Ph.D. degree in Education by carrying out research work under my guidance with honesty, sincerity and devotion. Dr. Pandey was a senior lecturer in English, but was promoted as a Principal of a Sr. Secondary School after completing his Ph.D. Amod has been working as senior lecturer in English with many other responsible posts in School. These two students were my favorite students – one as a research scholar for five years and the other as a very sincere N.C.C. Cadet for three years while doing his B.A.B.Ed. from our college in Bhopal. They kept inviting us to their place to meet their family members. My old colleague, Dr. Binod Tripathi had joined as Vice - Chancellor of the newly constituted National Institute of Teacher Education Institute at Banaras Hindu University (B.H.U.). Dr. Tripathi invited us to the engagement ceremony of his son. We thought of snatching the opportunity of visiting Kashi, formerly known as Banaras, but now called Varanasi via Rewa. Kashi is said to be the oldest city in the world.

We reached Rewa Railway station in the morning to find our students Dr. Pandey and Mr. Sharma with garlands to welcome us. Our accommodation was at the guest house of Sainik School Rewa, where we stayed for two days. Dr. Pandey took us to his beautifully constructed house, where we took our lunch prepared by Mrs Pandey. Dr. Pandey has two sons and one daughter. All the three children are well settled. Dr. Pandey and Amod took us for sightseeing, where we were thrilled to see the beautiful spring falling very deep in the river. Evenings were kept for Amod's family, where we enjoyed homemade dinner at his house. Amod has one son and one daughter, who are pursuing post Graduate courses. The next day, they took us to forest Safari, where we were fortunate enough to see white lions for the first time.

We boarded the evening train for Prayagraj (earlier known as Allahabad) and checked into our hotel at night. The next morning was reserved for religious fervor to have a darshan (sight) of the confluence of two prominent rivers namely The Mighty Ganges and Yamuna. We hired the boat and the boatman took us to the meeting point not only of two but three rivers – The Ganges, Yamuna and invisible Saraswati. This is said to be the most sacred point for Hindus. A lifetime dream came true by visiting Rewa and Prayagraj. After having darshan of the Ganges and having bath in the river, we boarded the Vande Bharata Train for Varanasi - the abode of Lord Shiva (one of the 12 Jyotirlingas) and the most sacred place for Hindus, 120 kilometer from Prayagraj. Prof Tripathi sent a car with a driver to pick us from Varanasi railway station and the guest house of IIT B.H.U. was already booked for us.

After taking evening tea at the B.H.U. guesthouse, the car dropped us in the highly crowded place of Banaras (Varanasi), where hundreds of rickshaw pullers were busy taking tourists from different parts of the world to the Kashi Vishwanath (Lord Shiva) Temple (56) in India. According to the legend, it was at this place that Shiva (The Hindu God of destruction) manifested as an infinite column of light (Jyotirlinga) in front of Brahma (The Hindu God of creation) and Vishnu (The Hindu God of preservation) when they had an argument about their supremacy. The first Jyotirlinga temple was built in the 11th century during the reign of Mughal emperor Akbar. It has been destroyed and rebuilt multiple times from 1211-1266 by two Gujarati merchants, Raja Man Singh and Raja Todar Mal. The temple was renovated with concrete platforms by Maharani Ahilya Bai in 1777. Maharaja Ranjit Singh ordered the temple's spires and domes to be covered in gold leafs in 1839.

There is another school of thought that the Kashi Vishwanath temple is said to have been originally built by King Vikrmaditya perhaps as long as 2500 years ago (57). Whatever be the origin of Kashi Vishwanath temple, it's the most sacred Jyotirlinga on the bank of the mighty Ganges with the popular belief that whoever dies at Banaras gets salvation. This is why many unknown bodies are flown into the river daily for salvation, but constantly polluting The Ganges. Sewerage of thousands of houses goes into the Ganges, which is another reason for pollution of such a sacred river for Hindus. The Ganges at Kashi is so popular that Hindus and foreigners from different countries keep thronging Varanasi 24x7 throughout the year from different corners of the world.

After walking through many narrow lanes crowded by religious tourists, we could reach the main deity in the evening and had darshan after rubbing our shoulders with an unending crowd of all ages throughout the narrow lanes. Touching Lord Shiva's ling was out of the question. We prayed to Lord Shiva to bless all our family members and every human being. The moment we came out of the temple, we again met a huge crowd for evening Aarti (prayer) on the bank of the river. There were thousands of boats, all having hundreds of people for the Aarti. We could also manage to board one boat in front of the Aarti site, which was continued for more than one hour by dozens of priests all in yellow robes praying for Lord Shiva and praying for the Ganges. The Ganga Aarti is very satisfying for all and one must attend the Ganga Aarti, whenever possible.

We returned to B.H.U. where a very delicious dinner was waiting for us. The next day was worship of Lord Visnhnu in Sanskrit language by the groom, family members and guests followed by evening dinner in the campus. Meeting Prof. Tripathi, Mrs. Tripathi, groom and family members filled us with great joy to keep us healthy and mentally fit for a long time with memories of our welcome by our old friend and two students and their families.

We face many ups and downs during our career. We may have all modern amenities at home, but meeting family members, relatives, friends and above all our teachers/students fills us with great joy to keep us healthy and mentally fit.

We also get the chance to meet our old students when they organize Alumni Get- Togethers. Two years back in July 2022, our many students of different batches arranged one such get-together in which more than 100 former students participated in the event at our college. Many came from the U.S. and one such was Raja Rangaswamy, whom I taught for one year. He joined an engineering college and shifted to America, where his sister Prema Rangaswamy, my senior during research work, lived with her family. We met many of my students after more than 40 years and started recalling the good old days. Many of them had retired after reaching the level of Principal. Most of them had become old but I was getting embraced seeing them touching my feet as a mark of respect. Some of them visited our home to pay their regards to Usha.

Another name coming to my mind is that of Deepa Gupta, B.Sc. B.Ed. four year course student and also my favorite N.C.C. Under Officer, who used to command the Republic Day parade in the college on 26th January. Some 7-8 years ago, she happened to be in Bhopal. Deepa visited us with her son Raghav and daughter Nidhi from Pune. Both of us were overjoyed to meet Deepa and her promising children.Deepa, Jasbir, Dr. L.N. Pandey, Amod, Dr. Amit Pandey, Dr. Sudhir Danej, and Dr. Jyoti Rathore keep sending us messages almost daily, which keeps us all happy and healthy.

Ajay has been working in America in the same hospital in Rome for more than 40 years. Ajay's younger brother, Naren after passing the Cost Accountancy Exam from the University of London in 1982 has the honor of working as CFO of many MNCs of America. Rashmi, my student at Bhopal and daughter of our family friend Col. J.S. Gulia, got married to Naren in July 1989 in Delhi. After marriage, Rashmi also joined Naren. My father-in-law Dr. Goel and Mrs Sarla Goel lived in an enclosed campus of Vikas Kunj near Janakpuri, Delhi till 2001. They were leading a very happy married life after the superannuation in 1984 from Indian Embassy Cairo, under the Ministry of External Affairs, government of India, New Delhi. They planned our trip to the U.S.A. in the summer of 1990, when we both had vacations from my college and her school.

Sarita, her husband MKG (M. K. Gupta), Usha Gupta and I left for America by Delta Airline via New York to Syracuse airport, very close to Rome. All our family members and our in-laws came to Delhi airport to see us off. A lifetime dream came true for me as I had never boarded an airplane before. After reaching Frankfurt in the morning, we changed the plane for New York. We reached New York at 12:30 pm after traveling for more than 14 hours from Delhi. We had a four hour layover before our flight to Syracuse. The aircraft was very small in comparison to our earlier huge airplane. The small aircraft started giving us jerks just after taking off, frightening us in the air and we started remembering our God to save us and help the flight to land safely at the Syracuse airport. We reached our destination after flying for 40 minutes. Collection of our bags from the conveyor belt was also a unique experience for us. We were thrilled to find Ajay, Pinki (Kavita) and their 2-year-old son, Arun, standing before us, while we were busy collecting our bags. We boarded the seven seater car of Ajay, which we had not seen in India by then. Our time for another surprise was when Pinki seated her son in a special seat fitted in the car, whereas we used to take our kid in lap while riding two wheeler. I occupied the front seat to the right of Ajay seated on my left hand side, while driving the big car. Another change in America as In India, we walk or drive to our left side on the road, but we were then driving on the right side of the road. We were getting newer and newer experiences in the U.S.A.

We were having a beautiful drive on very neat and clean four-lane roads from Syracuse to Rome with healthy green trees on both sides filling our lungs with fresh air. We seemed to float in the seventh sky with our car running at a high speed of 65-70 miles per hour and many more new experiences after touching the land of great America.

When Ajay and Pinki parked the car, we felt overjoyed to see that Ajay and Pinki have their own house and two cars because of their hard work in a foreign country. Pinki had made a very delicious dinner for us and we had a great fill after a long journey of about 24 hours. We had separate bedrooms. As we stretched on our bed at 9.30 pm, I was astonished to see the setting Sun through the window of the ceiling. What a great difference in time between India and America! As we were tired after the long journey, we had a sound sleep and got up at 5:30 am as usual. We took a shower (rather than taking a bath) and got ready for breakfast. In India, we generally eat stuffed paratha with butter and vegetables for breakfast. Watermelon, orange juice, and sandwiches were there for us, which we relished a lot. Whenever we used to visit Model Town Mansion (Delhi) of Kavita's family Delhi after her marriage with Ajay, we used to share happy moments with her father, late Murari Lal Gupta and delicious food prepared by her mom and Aunt.

When I was watching TV in the basement after taking a shower and breakfast, little Arun came running to me and asked me a question, "Have you not gone to the bathroom"? I couldn't understand and he kept repeating. Then he reframed his question, "have you not changed your night clothes?" Then I understood and it was a big learning for me that after taking a bath, we should change our clothes. Seeing me in night dress, the inquisitive kid of Goel family thought that I had not taken a bath (shower) and the little boy was confused to see me in the night gown.

We should change our night clothes after taking a bath/ shower in the morning to keep us fresh, healthy and presentable before family members and others to remain happy throughout the day.

Ajay left for hospital after taking breakfast at 7:30 am and Pinki to her office at 10:00. We kept ourselves busy by having a walk in the front yard and then glued to TV for local programs. We enjoyed our dinner with Ajay and Pinki before Sunset. Ajay and Pinki have a great bonding with a few Indian doctors. We had evening tea with Dr. Ramnani who was a student of Gandhi Medical College Bhopal in late sixties, from where our two daughters graduated in 1997 and 2002 respectively. Dr. Moza, a family friend of Ajay and Pinki, invited us for dinner at their residence. Lovely Arun always kept us happy with his poems and tantrums. After enjoying a two week stay in the beautiful nature of Rome town, and nearby areas for two weeks, Ajay and Pinky got our tickets booked for Dayton where our younger brother-in-law Naren was living with his wife Rashmi.

The recently wedded beautiful young couple was there at the airport to receive us. Both of them jumped with joy to see us and were welcomed by opening a Champagne bottle on arrival at their residence. Both Naren and Rashmi were employed in some companies and had their own cars. Naren always left for his office before we got up. Rashmi used to go a bit late after having breakfast with us. Naren was very busy in his company and always returned home after our going to bed. In a way, Naren worked for more than 12 hours almost daily due to the urgency of work or work culture of Americans. Now we can see our own children working almost for the whole day for their MNCs in Silicon Valley. This is the work culture of Americans that produces many Nobel laureates, innovators, and founders of many MNCs like Apple, Microsoft, Facebook, WhatsApp, IBM, Tesla, Space x etc. and NASA and thousands of many more.

Naren and Rashmi took us to the Air Force Museum, where we learned interesting stories of astronauts going to the Moon and Mars and many space engineers, who made America proud by many firsts to its credit. We recall our visit to the nearby city Cincinnati, where we enjoyed a very big cup of ice cream to our complete fill for the first time in our life exclaiming with joy, "Effluent America". Next weekend, Rashmi took us on a road trip to Chicago. On the way, she took us to Sea World where we were amazed to see various kinds of multicolored fishes and other aquatic animals in a very big aquarium, which was an eye opener and a beautiful sight for all of us.

Naren after finishing his work joined us and we were ready for our next destination in the beautiful city of Chicago. We were very eager to visit Dr. Ashutosh Gupta, maternal uncle of Usha, Sarita, Ajay and Naren. Dr. Gupta happened to be the physician of my ailing mother in the late seventies, during his posting at G.B. Pant Hospital and now working as a very senior physician in Chicago hospital. My mother continued his medicines till her passing away in 2001. On stopping the car, we confronted a very beautiful double storey white mansion welcoming us with Dr. Asutosh Gupta and his wife Dr. Nisha Gupta from Baraut – a town of the most populated Uttar Pradesh State in India. As we entered the house, we came across a very big elephant trunk in the drawing room, which was again a strange happening before our eyes as I had seen elephants only during my elephant ride after being awarded a National Merit Scholarship from the Government of India in 1962.

We three couples were allotted individual rooms with attached bathrooms on the first floor of the beautiful mansion. We enjoyed dinner with my maternal uncle, aunt and their two intelligent daughters and went for a sound sleep.

The next day we went to visit the beautiful city of Chicago with my aunt, where she helped us in purchasing one gold bracelet each for Usha and Sarita. In the evening Naren and Rashmi took us to the lake, where we were thrilled by the neat and clean water, surrounded by the constant sounds of the planes taking off and landing over us. After sunset, we were taken to the Chicago Tower. Our eyes got dazzled by the glittering light of the beautiful symmetrical developed Chicago City from top of the tower.

A memorable event in Chicago city with a beautiful lake and the Chicago Tower filling us with utmost inner happiness, courtesy of Dr. Asutosh Gupta, Dr. Nisha Gupta, Naren and Rashmi.

The next day, we left for Toronto to have a look at Niagara Falls – one of the Seven Wonders of the World. I was occupying the front seat with Naren. As we left from Chicago, we found six lane roads with green meadows and healthy green trees on both sides of the roads. Roads were very wide, neat and clean with no dry leaves anywhere. Cool breeze was blowing. I requested Naren to keep windows half open for us to inhale fresh and pure air in lungs to increase our longevity. After some time, all of a sudden we were astonished to see a few leaves lying on the road. Out of curiosity, I asked Naren the reason for such a change. Naren immediately said, "We are at the Canada border now". He stopped the car to get a visa from the Canadian government office on the border before entering the country. After driving for a few miles, we reached Toronto city and after 60 kilometers, we reached Lake Ontario, our destination. The beautiful drive on silken roads filled us with positive energy. We exclaimed our sincere thanks to dear Naren and Rashmi for a very comfortable drive.

Immediate expression of gratitude after any positive happening increases our happiness and the other party as well. Delayed reinforcer dilutes that.

Three rooms were already booked for us by Naren and Rashmi. After taking evening tea, we left with great desire to see the mighty Niagara Falls. As we came out of the apartment and started moving towards the fall, we found a large number of vegetable sellers sitting on the roadside giving us a glimpse of an Indian town. Water vapors coming from Niagara Falls were welcoming us with indications of the vicinity of the fall. Though our clothes were soaking, it was a memorable scene to see about 75,750 gallons of water (58) falling every second from the wide and very huge Niagara Falls. We had a great time in the evening for about an hour standing over there with the intention of taking a boat ride in the fall the next day as already planned by Naren and Rashmi. M.K.G., Usha, Sarita and I were amazed to see such a charisma of nature.

The history of Niagara Falls on the Canadian side (58) of the border goes back thousands of years, to the Ice

Age (About 12,230 years ago). Melting glaciers created massive lakes, including Lake Erie, which flew into Lake Ontario. The rushing waters carved out a river and eventually passed over the Niagara Escarpment, a steep cliff that runs from New York through Ontario. The water began to wear its way back up the river creating the Niagara Gorge.

The next morning, we walked towards the fall and boarded the cruise after putting on blue colored raincoats to protect us from rain of water vapors of the water flowing with tremendous speed from the Niagara Falls. The cruise took us somewhat near the falling water but still many meters away from the huge river managing million liters of water falling every minute. The Unimaginably beautiful sight of the blue colored water matching our raincoats. Cruise brought us back to the boarding site, thrilling us with joy and again expressing our gratitude to the young couple.

Naren asked us to occupy seats in his car for our next destination to Rome, the house of Dr. Ajay Goel and Kavita Goel for the second time. We crossed the Rainbow Bridge between Ontario and New York State on the American side. After driving for about 4-5 hours, we reached Rome in the evening where the little charming boy Arun welcomed us by jumping on our lap and having a warm hug with Ajay and Pinki. After doing full justice with dinner we all went to sleep with the idea of the next day's program in mind. Ajay told us in the morning about a boat ride in Lake George 130 miles away from Rome. We six adults and one 2-year-old child reached Lake George by traveling in two cars for two hours. Ajay had already booked three motor boats for us all. The boat ride undertaken in Lake George by our group in Rome some 34 years ago is very fresh in our mind since two of us (myself in one boat and Usha in another boat) increased speed of the boat on the turning point, which tilted the boat on one side almost flipping the boat had Ajay not cried from the third boat to reduce the speed. We were saved from drowning by the grace of God and the immediate sight of Ajay on us. However, helicopters with swimmers were hovering over us in the sky to handle any such mishap. Naren and Rashmi left for Dayton the next day to join their duties in their companies at Dayton.

All persons in foreign countries work for five days from early morning till late evening and go for outings on the weekends. Ajay and Pinki had already planned for our visit to Disneyland in Florida State. Disney World at Orlando is the tourist spot for various kinds of rides for people of all ages but especially for young children. There are cries of children and old people while taking such rides, but youths enjoy these rides and they keep having big laughter during scary rides. We could enjoy only a few simple rides but Sarita and MKG kept enjoying themselves with Ajay and Pinki. There are distances between different rides and one has to walk a lot to take all rides. After taking one ride, we were standing at a place waiting for our companions, when one American couple stopped near us, had a look on Usha, who had put on the saree, gold bangles in hands, gold earrings and a maroon colored dot on forehead as a sign of marriage for Hindu ladies and for long life of husbands. After looking at Usha from top to bottom, the couple exclaimed with joy, "You are a very elegant, complete lady". We both were wonder-struck for a moment for such an encouraging comment, but overjoyed to listen to the praise of the dress of an Indian lady.

Thousands and thousands of people from all over the world visit Disneyland with their children and family members to enjoy various water rides, machine rides and merry go rounds of different levels to test stamina and condition of their heart. Animation section was also quite astonishing to see artists working for many hours a day to develop one character. Mickey Mouse of Mickey House was one of the most favorite of visitors.

We returned to Rome with Ajay, Pinki and our most loved child Arun after our three days of very enjoyable tour of Disneyland, where one gets acquainted with many new scientific principles of controlling speed, brakes and getting over the roundabouts during the sliding heartbreaking rides. I was astonished to ask a question on the screen of a television without any person, but getting the answer very quickly. Another occasion of my surprise !

Our departure was in the first week of July. We made a few purchases for family members and my college friends from New York, where Ajay took us to suspension Bridge, World Trade Center Towers, Manhattan, and Statue of Liberty. World Trade Center having two towers of 103 storey was the highest tower of the world at that time (1990). The lift took only 53 seconds to reach 101st floor, where the visitors could go and take photographs from the tallest building and to have a look over New York City. We both, Sarita and MKG were extremely happy to visit Dayton, Cincinnati, Sea World, Chicago, Chicago Tower, Niagara Falls, Disney World, New York, glittering Manhattan, Lake George and the beautiful and serene town of Rome with Ajay, Pinki and Arun. Usha and Sarita could also celebrate Raksha Bandhan of love and affection of brothers and sisters by tying Rakhi on hands of their brothers, sister-in-laws and nephew Arun.

We took a flight by Delta Airlines and reached Delhi and our home town with sweet memories of our in-laws and gifts for our family members. Our parents had come all the way from Sonipat to Bhopal to look after our three college going children Bobby, Gudia and Dolly in our absence. Our son, Bobby came all the way from Bhopal and he reached the airport with his maternal grandfather to receive us at Delhi airport.

We got more chances to visit the U.S.A. in 2015, 2017, 2021- 2022, 2024 after shifting Bobby, Shuchita , Kunal and Aryan to America. By our next visit we tried to understand culture of western America by visiting San Francisco, Oakland, Los Vegas, Los Angeles, San Diego, Orange County, New York, many Universities besides UCB and Stanford, offices of Apple, Microsoft, Facebook and WhatsApp, Redwood forests, the Golden Gate Bridge and Bay Bridge of San Francisco. We were depressed to see Ground Zero in place of two high rising towers of the World Famous World Trade Center, which were bombarded and demolished by aerial attack by terrorists on September 11, 2001.

The sight of Ground Zero brought despair, pain and depression due to the criminal acts of terrorists, who, perhaps, don't believe in humanity. But above all this is gratitude, respectfulness, and love for the nation, family values, and care for others, which bring peace, happiness and ultimately good health to us all.

During our latest visit to San Francisco in June-August 2024, Bobby and Shuchita took us to their recently purchased farmhouse, from where we could pluck almonds from a few trees and grapes from a few crippers for family members and friends. Bobby and Shuchita also hosted a few parties for a few families and we also enjoyed parties hosted by their billionaire friends living in palatial houses. We also got chances to acquaint ourselves with many engineers who migrated to India just by taking only 8 U.S. dollars with them in the sixties, but now managing many MNCs. Aryan took us round his university of California at Berkeley. The Pizza Party at Bobby and Shuchita house was unique in the sense that Aryan prepared pizzas of different kinds for 20 guests single handed standing for 4 hours before the fireplace to help guests for his preparation.

Family plays the most important role in our life. Respect to our parents and grandparents gives us inner happiness. Friends contribute a lot in our life by helping us whenever we face any type of problem. Relatives are our extended family members. Meeting them off and on helps us in recalling good old days spent together, which again fill us with joy. We also get chances to visit

new places, which help to increase our horizon. Let's be respectful to all.

Can we think a while how we can help our children to understand the importance of family, relatives and friends by following a few activities given below:

1. Fade away status, wealth and ego and talk to the level of the opposite party.

2. Pay attention to others and listen to them carefully, without interrupting them to prove superiority.

3. Start caring for others more than yourself.

4. Remember the old saying , "More you give, the more you get".

5. Visit people in distress and help as much as we can.

6. Being respectful to others, we turn into very polite persons, which help us in becoming useful citizens of our community, nation and the globe.

7. Avoid road overtaking out of turn.

8. Read this chapter once again.

CHAPTER-12
RELIGIOUS PLACES, OLD AGE HOMES AND ORPHANAGES

Religion of a person is a personal affair. One may be very religious and the other may not be. If the community respects a religious person, the same should be the parameter for the one not following any religion, because the humanity of a person is the value of highest order to keep everyone happy and mentally fit. Wherever we go in India, we find temples, mosques, Gurdwaras and Churches visited very sincerely and regularly by large numbers of people in the morning and evening. There are many followers of 2500 years old Buddhism and Jainism, whereas Hindu religion is said to be more than 5000 years old. The difference in number of visitors depends upon followers. Visits to our religious places fill us with joy and inner happiness of mind. We get eternal peace of mind by praying to God with pure heart for the good health of our family members.

Due to the decrease in the joint family system, people of old age face many kinds of health issues and there is no one to take care of them. Some philanthropists open old age homes for care of such elderly persons. Some city councils also run a few such centers. In olden days, there used to be inns or dharamshala (living places for travelers), but with the passage of time and more developments, such places have become obsolete due to non-availability of care takers.

We may see many people going to old age homes to distribute food, fruits, sweets and clothes for residents of such homes to bring cheers on the faces of the elderly persons. Many people also visit hospitals regularly to distribute food packets, sweets and water bottles for attendants of patients coming from faraway places, and who can't cook food.

Some children lose their parents at a very early stage or some become orphans due to death of their parents in accidents, due to acute diseases or some mothers get rid of the newborn due to social taboos in some communities. Such unwanted or left over children have orphanages as the only places for bringing up those kids. Though there is an arrangement of food for such children in centers, many god fearing people go to orphanages on special occasions to help children living over there by donating cash, clothes, medicines and books to help the helpless children. All these places are the centers of happiness because we bring happiness on the faces of needy members of the society and happiness is bound to come to us in return.

Religious places are said to be the abodes of some super souls, where we get eternal peace by recalling their acts for humanity in their times by sitting and chanting mantras in praise of our God in temples, Gurdwaras, and mosque, or lighting candles in church and listening to sermons of the priest with utmost attention. Jains and Buddhists worship in their own ways. Ways of worshiping different gods of different religions may differ but the ultimate preaching and destination of all religions is the same, i.e. help to the needy and persons of weaker sections of the society, in whose bodies also God exists. At many places, thousands of devotees are seen visiting the religious sites, especially during special occasions presenting a positive picture of get- together, socialization and merry making of people bringing cheers on their faces.

India with a population of 1.44 billion people living in 28 States and 8 union territories distributed over 785 districts (59) is a great country of unity in diversity. People of India speak 122 major and 1599 other languages (60) with Hindi as the official language and Sanskrit as the oldest language said to be 7000 years old. Majority of Indians are Hindus and are followers of Hindu religion. India is a secular and democratic country, where God fearing people of all faiths live very peacefully following their own religion. In every small or big village or town, we find Hindu temples. In big cities, we may find a temple in almost every colony. Big businessmen or wealthy people construct temples. Hindu religion being very popular, temples are widely seen almost at every nook and corner of the city. Lord Vishnu, Lord Ram, Lord Krishan, Lord Shiv, Lord Ganesh, Lord Hanuman, Goddess Durga, Goddess Laxmi, Goddess Saraswati, Goddess Parvati and hundreds of semi gods are very popularly worshiped by Hindus and their temples are widely seen throughout India and in foreign countries.

India is very fortunate to have 12 Jyotirlingas. They are temples where Lord Shiva is believed to have appeared as a column of fire, hence called Jyotirlingas. They are situated at 12 places of India namely Somnath in Gir Somnath, Gujarat; Mallikarjuna in Srisailam, Andhra Pradesh; Mahakaleshwar in Ujjain, Madhya Pradesh; Omkareshwar in Khandwa, Madhya Pradesh; Baidyanath in Deoghar, Jharkhand; Bhimashankar in Pune, Maharashtra; Ramanathaswamy in Rameshwaram Island, Tamil Nadu; Nageshwar in Darukavana, Gujarat; Kashi Vishwanath in Varanasi, Uttar Pradesh; Trimbkeshwar in Nashik, Maharashtra; Kedarnath in Rudraprayag, Uttarakhand; and Gharishneshwar in Aurangabad, Maharashtra.

The above Jyotirlingas of Lord Shiva are the most sacred places. Every Hindu family of India or of any foreign country wishes to pay visits to these holy places in life time for taking blessings of God Shiva. We both visited Mahakaleshwar many times with Bobby, Shuchita, Gudia, Dolly, and our grandchildren. We could also visit Somnath, Nageshwar, Ramanathswamy in Rameshwaram, Mallikarjuna, and Kashi Vishwanath to take blessings of Lord Shiva. Whenever we went, we found huge crowds of pilgrims with the scene of a great fair with religious fervor all around. We got positive energy, eternal peace of mind, utmost satisfaction, fulfillment of our desires and extraordinary cheerfulness every time. By blessings of Shiva we both, our children and grandchildren are enjoying good health and leading a very healthy and happy life.

In my opinion, 12 Jyotirlingas are abodes of light of Shiva and visit to any one of Jyotirlinga fulfills the desire of devotees besides receiving blessings

for good health, happiness and prosperity. Any person of any caste, creed and from any nation can take blessings of God Shiva for good health and happiness by visiting Jyotirlinga with pure heart, if one so desires.

Badrinath, Kedarnath, Yamonotri and Gangotri are other four religious places situated in Uttrakhand for Hindu pilgrimages on the Himalayan Mountain range. These places are covered with snow in winters. They are open from 2nd week of May to the last week of October before the start of winters and heavy snowfall. Millions of devotees pay visits to these religious places. Economy of Uttarakhand depends upon tourists to Char Dhams (four religious places). But over use of land by greedy businessmen and politicians by constructing hotels on sloppy mountains is spoiling the ecosystem of Himalayas resulting in landslide and floods resulting in huge devastation of property and loss of life of thousands of people as mentioned earlier. But even then people don't take any lessons from natural calamities due to their immense faith in our religious places.. The state government is also not lagging behind to fill their treasuries from the visiting tourists in large numbers and not taking strict measures to control flow of tourists. We were lucky enough that we could visit the holy temple of Badrinath in 1986 with our father and family of younger brother, C.P. Gupta, working at RBI and posted at Kanpur at that time.

Amarnath Yatra in Pahalgam hill station of Anantnag district of Jammu and Kashmir state of northern India is also a very popular religious destination for

Hindus. There is a cave in which develops the snowy idol of Lord Shiva on the full moon of July- August (Shravan) month. The cave is situated on Baltal Amarnath Trek. The journey is very tedious, involving a trek from Pahalgam, spanning about 36 kilometers in 3-4 days (61) by stopping in camps on the trek route. However, Baltal route is shorter, covering around 14 kilometers, but still tougher. Thousands of devotees perform this religious journey during these two months. The authorities have now started providing helicopter service to pilgrimage to save their time and to make the journey a bit comfortable.

Another very popular religious shrine in Jammu and Kashmir is that of Goddess Vaishno Devi, another form of Goddess Durga, for which Indian Railway trains take tourists up to Katra (the extended station after Pathankot). The trek from Katra to the shrine stretched for 14 kilometers with mountain on one side and the deep drenches on the other side was very dangerous and tedious earlier but now made comfortable for pedestrians. Vaishno Devi, is very deeply and religiously worshiped throughout India. There are three Pindis (oval shaped idols), where Goddess Durga is worshiped in the form of these idols. There are multiple versions of the history of Vaishno Devi (62) but many agree that the shrine is almost 700 years old. Some legends say that Vaishno Devi was a devotee of Lord Vishnu who took a vow of celibacy. One day, Bhairon Nath, another god, saw her and chased her. During the chase, Vaishno Devi became thirsty and shot an arrow into the ground, causing a spring to gush out. She then rested at a place called Charan Paduka.

We happened to visit Vaishno Devi for the first time with our in-laws in 1970 and with Bobby, Gudia and Dolly and our brothers' families children in 1982, and with Bobby, Shuchita, Kunal and Aryan in 2008. Whenever we visited the shrine, we got immense pleasure and inner happiness of high order. Serving girls under 10 years of age with Prasadam (Halwa and Poori or pudding) made from wheat flour and pure ghee (molten butter) after darshan of the shrine outside the temples is always a great satisfying moment. In 1973, about 10,000 visitors were visiting the shrine daily but this number increased to 9.4 million (63) in 2023. The shrine is visited 24x7 throughout the year due to better facilities, easy sloppy but plain road, and provision of helicopter service from Katra to Sanjichhat. Devotees keep climbing the road in groups chanting songs of Goddess taking breaks on the way at Ardhkuwari to Sanjichhat. There are provisions of free Prasadam at 2-3 places for the comfort of tourists. A tourist from Delhi can return home in two days by taking the night train after having darshan of the Goddess.

Jagannath Puri, the temple of Lord Krishna, His elder brother Balram and sister Subhadra situated in Odisha state of India is a very famous shrine visited by Hindus and persons of other religion as well having faith in Lord Jagannath, whose name itself means caretaker of all humans on earth. We both visited this huge temple two times- once in 2018 with Urmila and Sarita and again in January, 2024 with Bobby and Shuchita. There is always a big crowd of thousands of devotees to have darshan of Lord Jagannath Ji., but presence of dear Bobby and Shuchita during our second visit made our journey and Lord's darshan very satisfying in spite of a very big gathering from different parts of the world.

There are thousands of other religious places in all parts of India not only for Hindus but for devotees of other religions. Kamakhya Temple in Assam, Tirupati Bala ji temple in Andhra Pradesh, Sai Temple in Nasik, Nath Dwara near Udaipur and many more are largely visited by devotees of all religions from all over the world. Golden Temple Gurdwara in Amritsar is the holiest place for Sikhs, besides thousands of Gurdwaras in India, Australia, U.K., America and many other countries. More than 50,000 devotees visiting Golden temple daily get free food in the form of Prasadam. All Gurdwaras are always open for free food and relaxation. Such type of help to humans of any community is rarely observed at other places. Gurdwaras are equally visited by persons of other faiths, but visitors are asked to cover their heads with a piece of cloth. Durgiana Temple adjacent to Golden Temple and Ramsar are other shrines in Amritsar.

Kurukshetra, famous for the Mahabharat (The Great Fight) fought between Pandavs and Kauravs, is famous for Lord Krishna's sermon to Arjun before the start of war. Lotus Temple of Delhi is the temple of Art without any statue or idol of any God but the most peaceful site for meditation to get peace of mind and inner happiness. Lord Ram temple in Ayodhya, Brahma temple at Pushkar in Rajasthan, Akshardham In Gandhinagar, Delhi, New Jersey and Orange County in America, Lord Krishna temple in Mathura, Vrindavan in Uttar Pradesh, and in Dwarka,

Iskcon Temples in Mathura Vrindavan, Sunnyville (USA), Sydney and at many other places of the world are other widely visited shrines by Hindu devotees. There are thousands of Hindu temples in the U. K., Australia, New Zealand, UAE, Nepal, Sri Lanka, Bangla Desh, and many other countries for getting peace of mind with inner happiness.

We also got a chance to visit Notre Dame Cathedral of Paris and Saint Mark's Basilica of Venice to pay our respects to Christ. Paintings on the walls of the cathedral were eye opening. We were amused to see the sitting arrangement for devotees to listen to the sermon of the priest. Protocol of proper dress for males and females is followed in churches too, which we liked a lot. Thousands of churches are there all over the globe for Christians and visitors of other faiths to take blessings of Christ. Bobby, Shuchita and Aryan got a chance to visit a more than five hundred years old cathedral undergoing renovation for the last 150 years in Barcelona in August 2024. An unique experience by them after visiting the old Cathedral over there.

Mosques of Madinah and Makkah in Saudi Arabia are very sacred places where millions of muslims visit their holy places from different parts of the world. We got a chance to visit the newly constructed Masjid at Abu Dhabi, where we had to put on black gown before entering the mosque. We liked their system as every religion has its customs and we must follow and respect their customs, if we are secular in mind. While serving at Ajmer College in Rajasthan, we visited Ajmer Dargah many times with our heads covered with a towel and paid our respects and prayed to God over there for the welfare of our children and family members. Our family members and relatives also felt happy after visiting Ajmer mosque, besides visiting the lone temple of Lord Brahma, the creator of the universe.

All religious places are abodes of super souls belonging to different sects. Every religion preaches for love for each other, especially for the downtrodden. They also advocate for truth , friendly and respectful behavior towards everyone, especially for our elders for their blessings to keep us always healthy and happy. Every religion is against violence. We can lead a healthy and happy life by following these values and by respecting all religious places.

Old age in developed countries is generally considered after 65 years when transition from middle age to old age starts. In India and other developing Asian countries, this transition may start a bit early when people start retiring from their active service and become entitled for Senior Citizens' facilities. By this time, most people attain freedom from daily chores and family responsibilities. Children settle in life by finding some job or starting their own business or some start up, get married and have their own children thus enabling Senior Citizens the honor of becoming grandparents. Persons taking their care from the very beginning by doing exercises, having healthy diets and having good relations with family members, relatives and friends remain generally healthy, strong and stout even after attaining the age of 65 years or more. But some people are not lucky enough and they start facing health problems. Some of them develop many diseases due to malfunctioning of our organs and old age becomes a curse for such elderly people.

Lucky are those persons who live with their children and grandchildren at this age and they have a good pass time, as is popular in some Indian and South Asian countries, where they get all types of assistance, when needed from their family members. With fast changing trends all over the world, such a family system is rarely seen as everyone in the family is over busy these days. People are becoming self centered and senior citizens start feeling neglected. Old people also understand the busy schedule of their family members and avoid sharing their health problems with them and their health starts deteriorating. In some cases, even very caring children and grandchildren start thinking about making some better arrangements, where someone can take care of them. Concept of "Old Age Homes" is very common in developing countries, where old people prefer to join such homes after selling their own home for better care. There they get proper attention by the caretakers, nursing staff, doctors and timely healthy meals. Library facilities keep them fresh for knowledge and simple games keep them fit. Such Old Age Homes are also coming up in small towns and cities of developing countries making life of old people worth living and comfortable, without troubling their busy children and grandchildren. They celebrate their birthdays, give calls to their family members, attend prayers in the morning and evening and gossip with inmates.

Some old age homes are run by city councils or municipal committees and some are run by philanthropists. We visited one such old age home in Bhopal, where one middle aged couple runs such an old age home under the name "Apna Ghar" (our own home) in a three story building with lift facility. About 20 old people were living there, each having his individual bed, bedding with very neat and clean bed sheets, pillow and the blanket. All elderly people living over there seemed to be very happy and shared their stories with us. They were served tea in the evening, which was shared by us too. Apna Ghar doesn't charge any fee from the residents. The expenditures are met out of the pension of a retired police officer, who happens to be the father of the lady running this center. We had taken some kitchen items for the center and our friend also donated grocery items. We also donated some cash for which receipts were given to us. Many more people keep donating kitchen items, vegetables, spices and cash to keep the old age home running very smoothly. The owner never faced funds crunch. The couple was involved in this strenuous task of managing 20 elderly people. Brother of the lady was a professor in a local medical college. A team of young doctors and nursing staff also take rounds of the old age home as per their convenience to check the elderly persons. It was a very satisfying experience to visit such a very well maintained Old Age Home. We were amazed to see the meticulous functioning of the old age home by social service to elderly people by the middle aged couple.

All old age homes are not goodie goodie. Many old age homes are run by charging fees from every elderly person. The owners are very greedy and are always in search of more money to earn more profit. They take two months advance as security from the person concerned or their family member, before admission with the condition of depositing the rent for the next month in the 1st week of the month. There are complaints about the quality of food and care of the senior citizens. In case of delay in making payment, the person is threatened to make alternate arrangements, because such greedy persons have nothing to do with humanity. Money and money is the only motto for them.

Orphanages (Anathalyas) are also run by city councils and private owners in the name of NGOs (Non-Governmental Organizations) to mint money and mismanaging Government funds. They have children from newborn to younger children of 18 years of age. Children of both sexes live in orphan homes. City councils, ministry of women and child welfare give grants to such centers. There is provision of food, clothing, education, permanent library, and their other daily needs. Such centers are in a way shelter homes for such children. There is provision for learning some vocations. Some children make full use of such a facility and many join colleges and universities after passing class X examination and developing some vocational skills. Many such children join the mainstream and keep doing well in their new community. Such bright children become brand ambassadors of their orphan homes and keep helping their old homes financially and doing community service in their old shelter homes where they were raised.

Visiting such places, rendering physical service and monetary help to residents of such needy children makes everyone happy. We can try to snatch such happy moments of life. One lady member of our relatives is very actively looking after an orphanage in Bhopal, where more than 50 children are being taken care of by lady members of the center. We got a chance to visit that orphanage 3 times and were highly impressed to see the development of children. Bobby and Shuchita are very closely associated with that center sitting far away in America, but they ensure to meet children and help them in kind and with cash, whenever in Bhopal and from America.

In some cases, there are complaints of sexual abuses in such centers, sometimes among the adolescent inmates and sometimes by male owners. Knowing it well, other residents keep silent out of fear from the owner, encouraging culprits to keep repeating such offenses. This is the negative aspect, but can be controlled by making a trust of the majority of female members and by regular meetings with inmates and sudden checks at odd hours. The Ministry of Women and Child Welfare can also control such incidents by becoming more vigilant for the safety and security of helpless children.

Arushi India (64) situated at Bhopal is a non- profit organization started by Anil Muggal in 1989 and cofounded by Rohit Trivedi, our four year course student (RIE BHOPAL), who was visually challenged and wanted some readers for preparing his lectures in

English after becoming a professor in a post graduate college of Bhopal. Anil and Rohit along with their three friends began recording audio books for 5 visually impaired school children, reading to the blind and raising funds to pay for the education of these children. Arushi started growing and now blossomed with more than 50 children of different disabilities. Since 1989, Arushi has grown to encompass work that develops capabilities in people with any disability and other groups of society who are marginalized from the mainstream. Kunal, passed out from UCB, and Aryan, a student of UCB have the honor to devote some time with inmates of an internationally recognized organization a few years back. We were thrilled to attend one musical program of Aryan and of about 30 children of different disabilities to sing, to act and to make the audience spellbound by their various performances. We were touched when our old students, Prof. Rohit Trivedi and Anil Mudgal welcomed us and others in the jam packed hall of the audience. The Bollywood film icon Gulzar is very deeply associated with Arushi- make the world one bit by bit.

A few of the following activities can make us happy:

1. We can have peace of mind and enjoy real happiness by becoming active members in organizing pilgrimages to different religious places.

2. We can also help old age homes and orphanages by paying weekly, monthly, quarterly or half yearly visits to such non -governmental centers and provide them financial help or by helping the organizers by gifting

them clothes, grocery items for the residents and may also spare some time to extend physical service.

3. It is rightly said that by making others happy, we actually make ourselves happy. Community service at such places is more rewarding.

4. We may come across many such centers where we can offer our services. Arushi at Bhopal is one such NGO, where many children with differently challenged abilities are stationed and doing very well in different fields.

5. Can we really try one or two of the above?

CHAPTER-13
MUSIC, DANCE & PAINTING

Music, dance and paintings are activities imparting inner happiness by following eudaimonic (65) approach by focusing on meaningful and self-realization and defining well-being or caring for others in terms of the degree to which a person is fully functioning. All these three are the arts of highest degree in which a person is totally absorbed, to create something new by constant meditation, practice and imagination. Imagination gives rise to innovations, but constant practice polishes the creation. These skills involve self realization, useful to self for getting happiness but also bring cheers and smiles to others by their creation. This approach of getting happiness and making others happy is different from the hedonic approach of happiness, when a person is always involved in seeking happiness only for himself without caring for others. Habits of good food, drinking, sex, winning an award fall in the category of hedonic happiness, which may impart happiness to self but not caring for others' happiness. We may come across many people in the society, who after getting an award become more proud and want to seek appreciation for themselves without caring for their peers or the community. We feel happy by having a refrigerator in our kitchen, AC in our room or the whole house, getting a four wheeler for the first time and so on, but with each material at home, we start wishing for more and more material of higher quality. By switching from an ordinary mobile to a smartphone, we become happier, but then we wish to have Apple mobile. If we have the i 11 model of Apple phone, then work hard to have i 12 and then the latest version, which keeps crowding the market with newer and newer gadgets, with no end in sight. Such types of personal achievements may keep one happy for the immediate moment, but more and more complexities start appearing in our mind, making us unhappy and confused. But real happiness is when we do something for others without any selfish motive.

People get happiness by chanting, singing and dancing alone or in groups, talking to each other, and sharing our ideas about many things which we don't know simply sitting at our place. People of all ages love drawing and painting based upon their understanding of matter and materials around us and using our imagination and creativity. These are the traits of high order. Burj Al Arab hotel of Dubai was designed by the imagination of an Australian architect in just 10 seconds as desired by the Sheikh of Dubai, and Prime Minister of UAE.

Ramtanu Padey, popularly referred to as Mian Tansen (66), or Sangeet Samrat, was a Hindustani classical musician in the court of Raja Ram Chandra Singh of Rewa State till 1562 and later as one of Navratnas in the court of Akbar (1562- 1589). Tansen used to keep the audience spellbound by his creation of Dhrupad compositions and many new songs. Tansen kept giving pleasure to his audience in the courtyard till his death on April 26, 1589 in Gwalior. This is 500 years old story of Music Samrat Tansen, but India is proud of many musicians of later ages and of our times of 20th century. Since childhood we have been listening melodious songs of Sangeet Sur Samragyee Lata Mangeshkar, Usha Mangeshkar, Asha Bhonsle, Kisore Kumar, Md Raffi, Shankar Jaikishan, Laxmikant Pyrelal, Alka yagnik, Udit Narain, Kumar Sanu, Sonu Nigam and singers of 21st century namely Shankar Mahadevan, Kailash Kher, Vishal Dadlani, Neha Kakkar, Diljeet Dosan, Arijit singh, Badshah and many more young artists. Indian TV channels are presenting many shows these days in which young singers entertain us by their singing traits under the mentorship of renowned judges. Millions of people of all ages watch these musical programs with great interest with family members and get enjoyment after daily chores before sleeping.

Ameen Sayani 67) transitioned from English to Hindi broadcasting gaining immense popularity with Binaca Geetmala. 30 minutes Geetmala program at 9.00 pm from All India Radio became every household program in India. The Show, airing from 1952-1994 with revivals in 2001 and 2002-2003, showcased Sayani's deep musical knowledge and revolutionized Indian Radio. "Namaskar Bhaiyo and Bahano, Mai Aapka Dost Ameen Sayani Bol Raha Hoon" resonated the voice emanating from the vintage radio sets, captivating living rooms nationwide. His style gained popularity when all India radio restricted the broadcast of Bollywood songs, becoming a platform for promoting simple Hindustani, in tune with audiences across India. After Sayani's death in 1991, people started listening to Vividh Bharti songs in the night from 10.00- 10.30 before going to bed, because the songs broadcast at that time and even now at other radio stations are always very lively and full of cheerfulness helping listeners to have a sound sleep. Such is the magic of music and its songs of different categories. We are also very fond of songs, which bring us inner happiness visualizing very deep meaning between the singer and the listener.

Music dissolves all barriers and binds the world together. That is why different musical Genres with diverse places of origin have influenced each other since time immemorial. The latest example is ED. Shreen in Kapil Sharma's show in India, singing a Hindi song in his own style on 18 May 2024 in Mumbai (69).

Musicians leave their footprints in the form of thoughts, words, and melodies of other musical genres like childhood friends exchanging toys. There have been great musicians, composers and singers all over the world. Every country small or big is proud of its singers, but Michael Jackson (70), Elvis Presley, Celine Dion, Lady Gaga, Selena Gomez, Shawn Mendes, Dua Lipa, Ariana Grande, Justin Bieber and Billie Ellish may be put in the category of 10 top singers (70) having huge following all over the world, besides thousands of others. Michael Joseph Jackson (1958- 2009) was an American singer, songwriter, dancer, and Philanthropist. He was known as the "King of Pop". He is regarded as one of the most cultural figures of the 20th century. Over a four decade career, his contribution to music, dance, and fashion along with his publicized personal life, made him a global figure in the field of art and culture.

Usha (71) is very fond of singing from a very early age. We listened to her beautiful songs after marriage and she kept singing songs during worship of God daily and during special occasions making all family members very happy. Her voice is very sweet and melodious. In October, 2022, we visited Newcastle to attend 10TH birthday of Ishana and 20th Marriage Anniversary of Deepika. Usha chose to sing a song on the special day before a huge gathering of more than 100 Indians and Australians. The song went very well with applause during the song and thereafter. Deelipka, Vineet and many of their colleagues appreciated the song a lot which motivated Usha to start singing as a hobby at the age of 73 years. Vineet himself is a singer of repute, besides being a G.P. of Edgeworth Family Practice at Newcastle (72). This was the turning point in Usha's life and after returning from Australia, she joined the singing class run by Mrs Nupur Ghosh (73) in our campus only. For the last two years, she continues to attend her class thrice a week and practice for different songs at home asked by her music teacher. She has now developed a passion for singing turning her into a very good singer at home and in monthly musical events of her Musical school. There is a positive change in Usha's personality bubbling with enthusiasm and increased level of confidence.

Bobby (74), Shuchita (75), living in the USA, Kavita (76) and Deepika (77) are also very fond of singing. The girls take regular singing classes at their respective places. I love listening to songs, but I'm not a good singer. While listening to songs, I feel like floating in space, and am a habitual listener to songs before going to bed. I go to sleep very fast after listening to a few songs and have a sound sleep. I think that Singing involves amalgamation of mind, body and soul and takes the singer to space, which is fathomless. This we observe when Aryan (78) sings the English song in his sweet voice with American accent with eyes closed, intensity of gestures and body movements keep the audience spellbound. Aryan has been learning singing for the last eight years in the church and presented many concerts in Europe in 2023 as a member of a choir group under the patronage of his music teachers. When our children join us at home, everyone participates in singing, spreading waves of happiness in all family members, which keep us all bonded among ourselves very strongly. When we are internally happy from the core of our heart, we get far away from worries and tension, improving our health to lead a healthy and joyful life.

I know the late Dr. P.T. Narsimhan (79), professor of chemistry, IIT, Kanpur, who loved music and singing regularly, besides being a passionate chemist of international repute at Kanpur. Prof. Narsimhan joined California Institute of Technology (Caltech) after retirement from IIT. Music was Prof. Narsimhan's abiding passion. We were lucky enough to have Prof. Nsarsimhan at our home once. He was a strong supporter of Indian classical music and was himself an accomplished flutist in the Indian Carnatic musical tradition, performing in India and later on in the United States, where he took his last breath, survived by his wife Leena and three children. Prof. Narsimhan was a renowned teacher, mentor, musician, thoughtful, insightful and a professor always to the point.

Students sitting till late night are generally found to listen to songs with ear pods for concentration to avoid sleep. This is the positive effect of music. However, some people become so much addicted to songs that they always keep using earphones, while walking or even while driving. They can't hear the horn of vehicles following them and they become victims of this misuse of earphones. Most of us like to switch on the song button while driving our car, bus, or a truck to enjoy the ride with music/ songs of their choice. Drivers ferrying their trucks to long distances drive with film songs to keep their focus on roads and avoid sleep during late night hours. Most of the sleeper coaches drive their night buses listening to songs of their favorite singer in low voice, but without earphones for the safety of passengers. These are the positive aspects of music. Singing and listening to songs are good hobbies to keep us healthy and happy.

Singing and dancing are very strongly attached to each other. Male and women in India and many other countries have been singing and dancing since time immemorial. No family function is complete without singing and dancing. Singing and dancing are an essential part of any cultural evening during annual functions of school, colleges and universities. Students participate in such events either in group singing /dancing performances which are always the source of great attraction for youths and the faculty members as well to keep everyone in high spirits. If singing improves the vocal cord taking the singer and the listeners to float in the seventh sky, dance helps in improving overall health of the performers by making legs, thighs, hands, shoulders and brain more active and strong. Birju Mahraj, Mrinalini Sarabhai, Rukmini Devi Arundale, Padma Subramanyam, Yamini Krishnamurthy have been international fame dancers of their time, whose popularity is spread beyond all boundaries.

Pandit Birju Mahraj (80), born on Feb. 4, 1938 (1938-2013) was an Indian dancer, composer, singer and an exponent of the Lucknow "Kalka –Bindadin" Gharana of Kathak dance in India. He also practiced Hindustani classical music and was a vocalist. He also worked with his uncle, Shambhu Maharaj at Bharatiya Kala Kendra, New Delhi and remained head for several years until his retirement in 1998. Mrinalini Swaminadhan (81) born in Madras, now called Chennai on 11 May 1918 (1918- 2016) was an Indian classical dancer, choreographer and instructor. She was the founder and director of the Darpana Academy of performing arts for imparting training in dance, drama, music and puppetry, in the city of Ahmedabad, where she devoted her last days. Rukmini Devi Neelkanta Shastri (82), born in Madurai on 29 February 1904 (1904-1986) was an Indian theosophist, dancer and choreographer of the Indian classical dance form of Bharata Natyam, and an activist of animal welfare. She espoused the cause of Bharata Natyam, considered a vulgar art performed by Devdasis in temples at that time. She sanitized and removed the inherent eroticism of Sadhir to make it palatable to India upper-caste elites. Rukmini Devi was the first woman in Indian history to be nominated as a member of Rajya Sabha, the upper house of Indian Parliament.

Padma Subramanyam (83) born on 4 February, 1943, in Madras, is an Indian classical Bharsata Natyam dancer. She is a research scholar, choreographer, teacher, Indologist and an author. She is very famous in India and abroad. Several films and documentaries have been made in her honor by Japan, Australia and Russia. She is well known as the developer and founder of the dance from Bharata Nrityam. Yamini Krishnamurthy (84) born on December 20, 1940 in Madras is an Indian dancer of Bharta Natyam and Kuchipudi styles of dancing and recipient of many Padam awards. Sonal Mansingh (85) born on 1st May, 1944 is a prominent Indian classical dancer who specializes in Bharatanatyam and is also known for Odissi dance. Nevertheless she is a social reformer, philosopher, Guru, Choreographer and trainer too. In 2003, Sonal was awarded Padma Vibhushan. She became the first Indian woman dancer to be honored by such a prestigious Award bringing happiness to her family, hundreds of her students and thousands of music lovers.

American singer Michael Jackson (70) was born on 29 August 1958. Michael was a great dancer besides being a great singer and the stage artist all over the globe. Through stage and video performances, he popularized street dance moves such as the moonwalk, which he named, and the robot. Michael will be remembered as the best artist of the 20th century as the artist attracting hundreds of thousands of his followers to listen to and watch his live concerts. Michael was so popular that all his concerts were always sold out. The largest attendance at a Michael Jackson concert (86) was at his free concert in Manila, Philippines on December 8, 1996 as part of the history Rizal Park estimated to hold a maximum capacity of 500,000 people. The last ever performance of Michael Jackson took place at the iconic Harlem Theater, The Apollo 7 years earlier to his death in 2009.

There is no age limit for learning to sing and dance. Many people start these hobbies even after their superannuation as a pastime and keep them happy in the company of music lovers or groups of dancers. I was overjoyed to see one 84 year old lady singing in the musical concert of Mrs Ghosh on 27tH April 2024 (87) at Bhopal, where Usha also gave her presentation along with 25 other singers. One of our friends, Dr. S.P. Sharma (88) started learning dancing at the age of 62 and also presented his performance on stage of RIE, Bhopal during the annual function in March 2006 at the age of 69 years in the jam packed hall of faculty members and students getting big applause from everyone. Dr. Sharma later started learning singing and continues practicing in singing and dancing. He is a regular morning walker and performs Yoga and exercises to keep him fit. Dr. Sharma, a friend of friends, always remains happy. He is always found cheerful with good health at the age of 87 years and an example for his peers.

Education and age is no bar for music or dance. The glaring example of Teejan Bai hailing from Ganiyari village of Durg district of Chhattisgarh state may be very inspiring for the readers. Teejan Bai (89) born in a tribal family on 8 August, 1956 is an exponent of Pandavani, a traditional performing art form, in which she enacts tales from the Mahabharata, with musical accompaniments. Teejan Bai learnt the art from her maternal grandfather, Brijlal, Pradhi even though the old man was very strongly criticized by the rest of the family for encouraging Teejan. Teejan Bai advocates for the preservation and promotion of traditional Indian folk music and culture of tribes of India. The Government of India honored Teejan Bai with Padma Shri, Padma Bhushan and Padma Vbhushan, India's highest civilian awards. Teejan had not gone to any school to get formal education. She learnt only to write her name in Devnagri script, but while in Japan for display of her art work, she was always addressed as Dr. Teejan as she received doctorate degree from a host of Indian universities. There are thousands of such artists found in many tribal districts of India who are promoting their art and culture with immense passion. Interested readers may visit Bharat Bhavan (90), Indira Gandhi Rashtriya Manav Sangrahalaya (Indira Gandhi National Museum of man) and State Tribal Museum situated at Shyamla Hills Bhopal for better understanding of art, culture and music of the tribal community of India.

Painting is another hobby which brings happiness to the painter and the onlookers. Painting involves imagination and creativity, which starts from an early age. That is why 2-3 year old kids are asked to draw anything in their notebook at the child care centers before making them learn numbers and alphabets of their language. One very interesting anecdote is worth mentioning for the benefit of readers. We had a painting competition for children on our campus as a part of annual activities. Children were divided in two groups – one up to 10 years of age and another from 10-16 years. Drawing sheets were provided by us and children were to make any painting of their choice. One 5 year old boy came running with a pencil in his hand and asked for a sheet. After 5 minutes, he handed over the sheet to us by drawing the picture of Lord Ganesh (one of the Hindu Gods found in every home) by imagining the picture kept at his home, worshiped daily in the morning and evening. That 5 year old boy got the first prize in his group, when he had not learnt much about reading and writing. This is the beauty of imagination and creation on a piece of paper. We come across many tribal males and females, who are expert in making paintings of their semigods and traditions depicting them on walls of their uncemented homes with thatched roofs without getting any formal education. Artists like Teejan Bai are found almost in all tribal districts of India.

Another great painting artist in our close contact is Vashu Jadhav (91), whose paintings are in great demand in India and abroad. She is so passionate about her work that in spite of her age related problem, she sits for hours together to put her imagination on canvas with unparalleled passion for painting work. Her paintings can be seen in drawing halls of painting loving owners and a few clinics of Newcastle. We are also very lucky to have one painting of the great artist in our drawing room. We were amazed to see one painting of an old farmer sitting in his rural attire at the artist's home. Painting is so big that while sitting in their drawing room, we get confused with a real farmer sitting in his field. Jadhavs have developed a beautiful farmhouse in the valley of hillocks of Sanchi town, near Bhopal famous for Sanchi Stupas of Gautam Budha. Onlookers have to salute such a passionate lady of clear thinking, imagination with creative art work, and always keeping herself cheerful.

Bhopal situated in central India is the epicenter of art and culture with Bharat Bhavan inaugurated by Indira Gandhi, the then Prime Minister of India on 13 Feb, 1982. Bharat Bhavan (90)is an autonomous multi- arts complex and museum, established by the Government of Madhya Pradesh with Charles Correa as its architect. The complex houses multiple art galleries, a graphic printing workshop, ceramic workshop, open-air theater, studio, auditorium, museum of tribal and folk art, and libraries of Indian poetry, classical music and folk music, where artists of different categories from all over the world give their presentation. Names of great artists like J. Swaminathan, Pandit Rajan Sajan Mishra, B.V. Karanth, Ashok Vajpayee, Girija Devi, Mohan Agashe, Lilleete, and many more artists of past and present are associated with Bharat Bhavan.

There are thousands of artists in different countries depicting their art in various fields, but Leonardo da Vinci (1452- 1519), Vincent Van Gogh (1853- 1890) and Pablo Picasso (1881-1973) are the world fame artists to be remembered for ever for their artistic work appreciated by people of all ages and making them happy by their creations. Leonardo da Vinci

(92), is widely recognized as the most famous artist of all time. He's the genius behind the Mona Lisa oil painting masterpiece, painted sometime between 1503 and 1519, while living in Florence. The Masterpiece painting is now hanging in the Louvre Museum, in Paris. It's considered as an object of pilgrimage by art loving people in the 21st century. The sitter's mysterious smile and her unproven identity have made the painting a source of ongoing investigation and fascination. The technique Da Vinci used in executing the painting left behind no visible brush marks, something that was said to make any master painter lose heart, making it truly a masterpiece. We were lucky enough to visit the gallery in 1991 and 2012 with Usha and Kunal, and were overjoyed to have a look at the world-famous Mona Lisa painting of Leonardi da Vinci. There we saw the craze of international art loving tourists waiting in queue for their turn to have a glimpse of the creation of the Mona Lisa even after 500 years of the artist's death.

Vincent Willem van Gogh (92) was a Dutch post-impressionist painter, famous and influential figure in the history of Western art. In just over a decade, he created about 2100 artworks including around 860 oil paintings, most of which date from the last two years of his life. Landscapes, still life, portraits and self-portraits of Vincent are characterized by bold colors, dramatic, impulsive and expressive brushwork that contributed to the foundation of modern art. Starry Nights, Café Terrace at Night, Sunflowers, Self Portrait and many more are some of the world-famous artwork of Vincent. Vincent wasnot commercially successful. He developed mental illness and committed suicide at the young age of 37. However, within the span of a century, van Gogh has become the most recognized painter of all time. There are many people like van Gogh, who get recognition after their death. Such artists make the public happy in their absence.

Pablo Picasso (93) born on October 25,1881 was a Spanish painter, sculptor, printmaker, ceramicist, and theater designer, but spent most of his adulthood in France. Among his most famous works are the proto-Cubist Les Demoiselles d'Avignon (1907), and the anti-war painting Guernica (1937), a dramatic portrayal of the bombing of Guernica by German and Italian air forces during the Spanish Civil War. All the above artists attracted huge crowds of their art lovers during their life period but more so after their death, because their works are widely appreciated by the art lovers and one is forced to think about their passion, imagination, creativity and even hardships of life but making all onlookers internally and externally happy. When we are mentally happy, we remain positive in our thinking to make us healthy and more joyful.

Singing, dancing and making paintings fill us with unique happiness. As there is no age bar for starting these activities in life, we may start whenever we get a chance. After learning these arts, we may help the community members to learn these skills to bring cheers on the faces of others and make ourselves also healthy and happy.

A few of the following activities can also make us happy by developing habit of singing, dancing, painting or some other one like Usha, who started singing at the age of 73:

1. Each one of us may have some hobby to pass time in leisurely moments, besides our main job. We may opt for any one out of music, dancing, singing, writing stories or any other of one's liking that leads to happiness.

2. There is no need to be an expert. Hobby is a pass time to remain busy and happy.

3. While choosing a hobby, one shouldn't think of competition. This is for self realization.

4. Hobby should be taken with ease and without any tension. Happiness and tension are opposite to each other.

5. Hobby shouldn't be taken at the cost of our health.

CHAPTER -14
PUNCTUALITY, REGULAR EXERCISES, SELF CARE AND ATTRIBUTES FOR JOYFUL AND HEALTHY LIVING

There is an old saying, "If You are Punctual, Half the Battle is Won". Punctual people never miss the bus. They are never late in school, college, university, office, and meetings. Doctors can't afford to be late in the operation theater for the safety of their patients and a soldier can never be late for a fatal operation for enemies. Farmers must plough the fields and sow seeds before the arrival of monsoons to get good produce from their fields. Mall owners are always punctual to start their work because it is rightly said, "Death and Customers Wait for None". Trains and flights mostly maintain their timings even after traveling for thousands of miles to become examples for others. Same is the case with post offices and banks to serve their customers on time. Officers and employees working in such bodies are punctual everywhere and this trait helps them to remain happy and to make others happy. A happy mind leads to good health.

I learnt the value of punctuality from my parents at the age of 5 years. Getting up early in the morning, worshiping God after taking a shower daily before leaving for school by running one kilometer to reach the assembly ground before ringing of the bell. Another activity of our daily routine was to come back to school at 4.00 pm daily after two hours after taking our lunch. This made me and my other classmates very fast in solving arithmetic problems quickly involving multiplication and division operations. Class five examinations were conducted by the district board of education in another school at a distance of about two kilometers. We used to go to the secondary school by walking with classmates from my village and never got late throughout the year. The same habit of punctuality and fast walking continued during my college and university days. Besides being punctual, fast walking has kept me fit till now at the age of 79+. Habit of walking from an early age doesn't make me feel tired even now after having a daily walk for about four kilometers.

After joining Teaching profession, I maintained my habit of punctuality throughout my career in Panjab University, Delhi Administration and Colleges of NCERT by reaching the classroom five minutes earlier than my time and waiting for the professor to come out of the class after ringing the college bell. I never took attendance of students to save time of my 80 students, by calling their names. Students used to write their names on a piece of paper, without putting a proxy on their friends. Saving time for students helped me always to cover one more concept in class of 45 minutes, with full understanding of the content, which made me their favorite teacher. But my punctuality made me somewhat unpopular with my peers, who used to be uncomfortable in my presence.

I followed the principle of punctuality throughout my personal life even while visiting friends, attending parties and during our travel plans. We were frequent travelers with our children at least 2-3 times a year by train and maintained this practice even now. During the last 50 years, we missed the train only once, even after starting 3 hours before the departure time of the train, though the distance from home to the railway station was only two hours. This happened due to traffic congestion that evening. The habit of punctuality is also inculcated in our children and grandchildren and they are also never late to reach their school, college, university or their offices. It's a matter of great satisfaction to us, which always keeps them healthy and happy.

Punctuality always keeps us healthy and happy, as we don't have any worries in mind. We reach our work place before time and remain carefree during our travels and later at our workplace. Punctuality is one ladder of success. If we are punctual, half the battle is won, and we remain mentally happy with good health.

There is another saying, "Early to Bed and Early to Rise, Makes a Man Healthy and Wise". We have been in the habit of getting up early in the morning since our childhood and have been following the same till date. We generally go to bed at 10.30 pm and get up at 5.30 am early in the morning. After finishing natural calls, I start doing deep breathing exercises for about half an hour followed by Kriya Yog and a few stretching exercises. Then a 2 kilometer walk on our campus keeps me fit for the whole day.

Usha also follows almost the same pattern besides supervision of kitchen work and assisting the domestic help. In the absence of domestic help, I help Usha with kitchen work. Working with Usha in the kitchen proves doubly rewarding for me first by releasing my tension by change of work and second by enjoying happy moments with her free, while being free from my college duty after my superannuation. While watching TV during the day, we keep taking a break after every hour and walk barefoot from our drawing room to the kitchen. Evening tea is followed by having a 2 kilometer walk again in our campus, meeting campus members to have chit chat with them, which keeps us happy.

We can defy anything, but we can't defy age. With the increase of age, we tend to invite health issues like hypertension, diabetes and many others, but these can be put under control by following a healthy lifestyle. A hot glass of water in the early morning avoids constipation. One glass of buttermilk during breakfast helps in digestion and one bowl of curd with green vegetables and dal at lunch and one glass of hot milk helps in keeping our bones strong. I am keeping fit in spite of having the above health issues, but I am very lucky to remain healthy and happy by my daily routine of walking, exercises and controlling my dietary habits, and by taking medicines very regularly.

There are many young boys and girls, who remain very busy in the office and glued to their laptop. Employees working in banks, railway reservation counters, post offices and other departments dealing with public meetings from morning till evening, with a very short lunch break can't afford to leave their seat even for 2 minutes due to the public pressure. They become victims of many diseases like shoulder pain, weak eyesight, numbness in leg, body pain and early over aging. Many of them are so busy that they don't find time for regular walking or exercises. It's observed that if we leave our seat after working on a laptop for about an hour just for five minutes, wash our eyes with cold water, stretch our hands and legs only for two minutes, and walk about 100 steps before returning to work, we will feel fresh and can avoid such diseases. Most of the offices are five days a week. We may reserve the weekend for getting up early in the morning, going for a long walk in some nearby park for doing light exercises and yoga. We may also plan visiting family members, relatives or friends or even going for nearby excursions. This will help in keeping us healthy and also making us more social, and joyful..

Women folk in any part of the world are hard pressed due to double or triple duties, they perform from early morning till late night. Mothers are the worst affected persons. They are to keep their children ready for school in the early morning, prepare Tiffin for children, husband, and herself, if she is also a working lady. The same cycle of work starts after returning from the office.

Some male members are very co-operative and help the working mothers. However, the majority of mothers keep working like machines without thinking about themselves. Such a busy schedule of working mothers results in their poor health leading them to become victims of various

diseases. Self care is the only medicine for such overburdened ladies.

Situation in developed countries is much better where both the partners take care of each other. They are actually working as two wheels of the cart, which was a very common sermon of an Indian priest at the time of marriage of a man with a woman, but very rarely practiced now only in a few families. This is causing disharmony in relations, daily fighting at home, making children violent and creating an atmosphere of sadness, unhappiness and increasing number of divorces and breaking of family relations. Some 50 years ago, divorce in India and other Asian countries was very rare, but it has become very common in India and other countries too. Situation is becoming very alarming all over the globe, which needs a serious thinking of lawmakers and elderly community members. The best way in the present scenario is to take care of self i.e. self care.

Caring starts from the very beginning. As a child is born, the mother starts caring for the newborn. If the mother is not serving, she takes care of the child at least for three years. Mother is the child's first teacher. She takes care of the child's every need by changing diapers, massaging, giving showers, and taking them to the park for Sun bath and fresh air to keep lungs in proper condition. The child starts responding by giving a smile after three months and mother keeps the child in good humor by singing melodious songs / rhymes to make him / her sleep fast. The child starts sitting after six months and waking after enjoying their 1st birthday. These are very happy moments for the parents. Working mothers have to send little children to child care centers, where all needs of the child are taken care of by caretakers and children start smiling, giving gestures and start expressing by gestures and then comes the stage of speaking.

As the children start growing, it is believed that learning skills of children are very fast. This is the stage, where lies the importance of parents, care takers and teachers to inculcate family values in them. They are taught to share their meals, their toys and their belongings with their peers. Here starts the most important value of sharing with others and taking care. As they grow old, they are acquainted with simple vocations followed by life useful vocations, which can help them in earning their livelihood. Swimming, playing soccer, learning music, singing, dancing, karate, even tree climbing, and many more activities are taught to children in pre - primary and primary schools besides giving them knowledge of alphabets and numbers. Starting from home, child care centers, pre primary schools till high schools, colleges and universities, children start learning many things useful in life, but the most important value is sharing and caring for others, which make one the most important citizen of the society.

As we grow old, we start facing new challenges in life. If we start taking care of ourselves from the very beginning following healthy lifestyle like walking, doing exercises, saving for rainy days, socializing, having some friends, who can be of real help in case of any diversity, then old age also becomes the period of enjoying life with a smile and making others also to smile. Life is mortal and every living being is to leave the world by perishing itself with soil, but people keep echoing their good deeds even after hundreds of years. To mention a few past or present everlasting names, we keep singing songs sung by Sangeet Samragyee Lata Mangeshkar, Usha Mangeshkar, Asha Bhonsle, Kishore Kumar, Md. Rafi, Jagjit Singh and hundreds of other singers and musicians. They have become eternal. Similarly Mahatma Gandhi, Jawahar Lal Nehru, Sardar Patel, Lal Bahadur Shastri, LalaLajpat Rai, Bhagat Singh, Subhash Chandra bose will be remembered by many generations to come to remember their sacrifices in getting India freedom from British rule. The great Indian poet Rabindranath Tagore, Great scientists like Albert Einstein, Newton, Praful Chandra Ray, Sir C.V. Raman and thousands of others are remembered with great honor and respect all over the globe for making our life more enjoyable, comfortable by their inventions. King Martin Luther is a common name in every corner of America for changing the lives of people brought from Africa by his strenuous efforts in making them equal in status by the right of one vote.

We are to take care of ourselves without expecting anything from others, because expectation from others leads to unhappiness. Society has given us a lot and we should try to repay something in return. Leading a joyful and healthy life involves a blend of physical, mental, and emotional well-Being. Here are some key attributes as per the opinion of citizens from different sectors of the society, which can help readers to lead a healthy and happy life.

A. Usha Gupta, (71) - A former English Teacher in Anand Vihar School, Bhopal for 21 years, bringing up three children and raising six grandchildren, and the House Manager since 1970 with passion of music suggests the following attributes for healthy and happy life in the family:

1. Respect the elderly family members without any bias and love the younger ones without any partiality.

2. Giving up ego and friendly conversation with all members creates an exemplary environment in the family to bring happiness to all.

3. While working in a joint family, the responsibility of sacrifice of elders is more for all members and readiness of service by younger ones towards elderly persons and respect to them makes a happy joint family.

4. Division of work in the joint family minimizes chances of quarrels among members, and all may avoid backbiting. Expressions of any displeasure or different opinion from others may be discussed with all and we should not force other members to agree to our proposal / thinking.

5. All members should speak the truth and inculcating values of truthfulness, punctuality, hard work, love for each other, respect to teachers and elderly persons, caring

and sharing with others in growing children will help them to become useful citizens of the society.

6. Respect for fair sex by male members always helps to develop a congenial environment around us.

7. Importance and habit of getting up early before Sunrise and physical exercises will be a milestone in the life of growing children.

8. one glass of buttermilk in the morning, one bowl of curd/yogurt during lunch and one glass of hot milk will keep all members healthy.

9. Use of seasonal fruits and leafy vegetables in daily diets along with some amount of carbohydrates is also very much desirable for good health.

10. Importance of neighbors and community members acts as a panacea for remaining mentally fit.

11. The importance of music, dance, painting and thinking out of the box leads to creativity.

12. Habit of getting ready for school by reading 3-5 pages of books of all subjects relieves school/college /university children tension free. Revision of school notes after returning home, helps in strengthening their understanding of concepts.

13. Emphasis of negative effects of junk food on our health helps in understanding the importance of a balanced diet.

14. Following Raat Gayi, Baat Gayi ((Forgetting Negative Happenings of the Day after the Night) proverb helps in keeping cordial relations in the family and everywhere. Old mishappenings, if any, should be forgotten and forgiving others is a great bliss.

15. Faith in our religion and faith in others' religion and trust in all family members, cordial relations with neighbors, community members and care and respect of workers at home or in the community keeps us always healthy and happy.

16. Self care is the best care for everyone. We can help others only when we are bodily healthy and mentally happy

B. Bobby (74) - A very energetic, enthusiastic, very social, and a friend of friends, young Engineer with global experience of many continents namely Asia, Australia, Europe and America, and now a Venture Capitalist and founder of AI companies in Silicon valley of America suggests the following attributes to lead a healthy and happy life :

1. **Balanced Diet:** Eating a variety of nutritious foods to fuel the body and maintain good health.

2. **Regular Exercise:** Staying active through activities we enjoy, whether it's running, swimming, yoga, or any other form of exercise.

3. **Adequate Sleep:** Ensuring get enough restful sleep each night to rejuvenate our body and mind.

4. **Stress Management:** Practicing techniques like meditation, mindfulness, or hobbies to reduce and manage stress.

5. **Positive Relationships**: Building and maintaining support and relationships with family members by visiting them and knowing about their welfare, health and their needs from time to time.

6. **Purpose and Goals:** Having a sense of purpose and setting achievable goals to give direction and fulfillment in life.

7. **Mental Health Care:** Seeking help when needed and taking care of our mental health through activities that boost our mood and reduce anxiety.

8. **Continuous Learning:** Keeping our mind active by learning new things and pursuing interests and passions.

9. **Gratitude and Positivity:** Cultivating a mindset of gratitude and focusing on the positive aspects of life.

10. **Giving Back:** Engaging in acts of kindness and contributing to the community can provide us a sense of fulfillment and joy.

C. Shuchita Gupta (75) - CTO (Global Health Care) IBM in the U.S. with a very wide experience of more than 25 years in technology, and a regular donor for charities defines happiness as that uplifting state of mind where positivity thrives, free from fear and stress, making us feel as light as clouds and lasting joy often comes from small moments rather than great achievements. The following attributes as conceived by Shuchita may be helpful to remain healthy and happy:

1. Whether it's a family holiday at the beach or anywhere else or admiring a beautiful flower in our yard in the morning, these simple pleasures can provide a profound sense of happiness that sustains us during tough times.

2. Connecting with friends gives us a sense of community, while cherished childhood memories - like sleeping under the stars or excelling in school - bring immense joy.

3. Giving back and uplifting others infuses life with meaning and fulfillment, and creating something new, whether through innovation or art, fosters a deep connection to our passions.

4. Acceptance is crucial for happiness, allowing us to navigate life with less stress.

5. Life is a boomerang; when we help or appreciate others, we actually cultivate happiness within ourselves.

6. Practicing gratitude keeps us anchored in joy, and generosity enhances our sense of abundance.

7. Forgetting and forgiving keeps friends and family members together with happiness.

8. Learning is a continuous process, which always keeps us free from tension and worldly affairs and with good mental health.

9. Self care, care of family members, relatives and friends without expecting anything from anyone and enjoying life within our means always keeps us happy and healthy.

10. For me, the happiest moments include family holidays, sharing achievements with parents, long drives with my husband, and the unparalleled sheer joy of witnessing the birth of my children.

Pray to God to Keep Everyone Happy !

D. Anand Chandeliya (94) - An eminent engineer living in Bhopal recommends the following attributes for leading a healthy and happy post-retirement life:

1. Avoid traveling alone.
2. Travel with a spouse.
3. Avoid going out during peak hours.
4. Avoid excessive exercise or walking.
5. Avoid excessive reading, mobile use or watching TV.
6. Avoid overmedication.
7. Visit doctors on time and take medicines regularly.
8. Avoid property dealings after retirement.
9. Always carry your ID and important phone numbers.

10. Forget the past and don't worry too much about the future.
11. Eat what suits you and chew slowly.
12. Be cautious in the bathroom and toilet.
13. Avoid smoking and drinking, they are harmful.
14. Don't boast about your achievements.
15. Travel extensively for a few years after retirement, then avoid crowded places.
16. Don't discuss your property and assets with others.
17. Exercise according to your capacity and health.
18. Avoid headstands and kalabati if you have high BP or heart diseases.
19. Stay positive and avoid excessive emotions.
20. Don't sleep immediately after eating.
21. Don't lend money to others.
22. Avoid giving unsolicited advice to the next generation.
23. Respect others' time.
24. Don't try to earn more if you don't need to.
25. Avoid day time naps to sleep well at night.
26. Have your own space and respect others' privacy.
27. Make a will and consult your spouse.

28. Avoid giving your retirement savings to the next generation.
29. Join a senior citizens' group, but avoid conflicts.
30. Don't disturb others if you can't sleep.
31. Don't pluck flowers from trees.
32. Avoid discussing politics, or accept differing opinions by saying, 'We agree to Differ'.
33. Don't constantly complain about your health.
34. Avoid quarreling with your spouse, as they are our primary support.
35. Attend spiritual events, but don't become a blind follower.
36. Live a stress-free life with a smile.

Courtesy : Dr. S.P. Tiwari, former Professor BHU, India.

E. Dr. Kavita Gupta Ghadale (76) - Senior Consultant and Laproscopic Surgeon, with more than 30 years of shining career as a popular doctor and now at Bombay Hospital Indore - 45010, India is of the following firm belief about women

"Respect and kindness towards females are essential values to uphold in our daily lives".

1. Listen actively and believe their stories.
2. Avoid objectification and inappropriate comments.
3. Support and amplify their voices.

4. Respect their boundaries and consent.
5. Stand up against harassment and discrimination. Foster a culture of inclusivity and empathy.
6. Treat women with dignity and equality.

This should always be remembered by all that respect is a fundamental right. Let's work together to create a safe and supportive environment for all ladies around us.

Kavita's following powerful ways may also be very useful for good health and happiness of everyone:

1. **Listen Actively** - Sometimes we don't listen to others actively. We may pay active attention with care to reduce miscommunication.
2. **Express Gratitude -** Thank those who have helped you, no matter how small is the gesture.
3. **Give genuine Compliments** - Sincere praise can boost someone's confidence.
4. **Surprise by smile gifts** - A thoughtful token can bring joy and joy to someone's heart.
5. **Spend quality time -** Share meaningful moments with loved ones - parents, children and friends
6. **Forgive and show empathy** - Let go of grudges and try to understand others' perspectives.

7. **Celebrate others' successes** - Genuinely rejoice in others; achievements.
8. **Volunteer** - Helping those in need and my patients bring cheers to me and my patients.
9. **Meditate and spread Positivity** - Share calming energy and inspire posi**tivity**
10. **Create something beautiful** - Share art, music, or writing that uplifts others.
11. **Offer words of encouragement** - Support someone facing challenges.
12. **Be Present** - Give full attention to the moment and those around us.
13. **Practice random acts of kindness** - Surprise people around us with selfless acts to make them happy.

F. Dr. Vineet Jadhav (72) - CEO of Edgeworth Family Practice Newcastle with more than 27 years of experience in India and now at Australia suggests the following attributes to his patients and others to remain healthy and happy:

1. The body is like a fantastic machine, with an infinite amount of complexity. Treat it with respect.
2. Our body is our true possession in our life. Look after it.
3. Our body is our vehicle which carries us from birth to the end of life. We have only one. take care of it.

4. Nature / God has created our body with all the means of repairing and healing itself. Learn how to assist it in doing so, rather than hamper it.

5. Our body is designed to sustain itself with the most minimal of requirements. It needs water to run, fresh air to breathe, some food and sleep. Let's give at least all these to keep it fit.

6. There are 1,440 minutes in a day, of which we sleep almost half of it. Our body just needs the minimum of 30 minutes of exercise to keep it healthy. Can we give this a little bit?

7. People want to live long but don't think how they can reach that age. Out of 100, only two people reach the age of 85 years, but one of them celebrates their birthday at home and the other one in the nursing home. Both have achieved longevity, but only one has retained quality. Modern science and medicines can increase longevity but can't improve quality. This is in our hands.

8. When our body does exercise it experiences pain, but it's the pain which releases chemicals and hormones in our body which rejuvenates it. The soil in the field is broken and tilled. Only then can crops grow on it.

9. Happiness is just like a butterfly. The more you chase it, the farther away it flies from us. It's only when we are still and quiet that it comes to us.

10. Try to see a Sunrise or Sunset at least once in a week or daily. if we can't see it from where we live, let's expose our body to this light frequently. It restores our pineal glands in our brain to produce melatonin, a hormone that regulates sleep and wakefulness.

11. Learn how to breathe and control properly. We can achieve mastery in this technique by constant practice.

12. Drink the majority of water intake in the first half of the day. The body hydrates better in this way.

13. The need for sleep changes true life. Try to get a major part of our sleep from 12 O'clock to 4 am in the night. By doing so, our body functions better.

14. Try to understand the difference between exhaustive sleep, drug induced sleep and true sleep. True sleep always invigorates us and wakes us up feeling fresh.

15. Don't chase success but chase failures, when you find it. Analyze it, dissect it, and learn how to overcome it.

16. The brain is like the hardware of the computer and the mind is like the operating system which runs it. When we are born, there is a very basic program in our minds. It's what we learn through our life which determines how useful or good our mind is. So we need to be careful of what program we enter in our brain.

17. The default program of our mind is to remember negative or traumatic events. That is why it's always easier to remember bad things. Being positive requires us to train our brain to identify and remember the good things. It's hard work !! but worth it!

G. R.M. SAHU (95) - An engineer of Bhopal suggests following 10 golden tips for Happy Seniors:

1. Early in the morning if we are woken up by our alarm clock, mobile phone, birds chirping or other noises, be happy and count yourself blessed. it means we still are part of this world.

2. After waking up, drink some water, text people you know, love and care for. Greet them with "Good Morning". It means we can think clearly and we are healthy. We can start a new and beautiful day.

3. If we receive text messages and calls from friends inviting us to have meals together, or spend time with friends, it means we are friendly and have good relations with people. Friends are still thinking of us.

4. Occasionally, some people may speak ill of us or gossip behind our back. It means that still we are a very important person in their hearts.They are certainly not doing as well as we in life. We should feel happy and blessed.

5. If we worry about being overweight, we are eating very well, and our meals are sumptuous and full of nutrients. Don't worry. All health talks on healthy living, and strong immunity

are based on food. Just exercise, control and everything in moderation.

6. If we often go out with friends, eating, chatting, traveling, seeing places and have a change in our environment, it proves that we have some standards in our way of life.

7. If we have a good sense of humor, it means we are young at heart and we are very healthy.

8. If we have passed 65, be happy and be content. According to a world survey, only 8 out of 100 people live past 65 years old.

9. If we can go out and buy ingredients and cook; we see well; we hear well; know how to use our mobile phone to send text messages; write about our memories; write a story; count yourself very blessed and have a very successful life.

10. If we are reading this message with friends, it means that we are not selfish, we are kind hearted; and we are a person who cares and loves human kind.

H. Mukesh Sahni (96) - Former SSP in CBI and living in our campus suggests the following tips to improve our sleep quality:

1. Establish a bedtime routine - Develop a calming pre-sleep routine, such as reading a book, taking a bath, or practicing relaxation techniques like meditation or deep breathing.

2. Stick to a sleep schedule - Go to bed and wake up at the same time everyday, including

weekends, to regulate our body's internal clock.

3. Create a sleep - conducive environment - Make your bedroom a sleep heaven by ensuring it's dark, quiet, and cool. consider using earplugs, blackout curtains if necessary. Invest in a comfortable mattress and pillows.

4. Limit exposure to screens before bed - The blue light emitted from smartphones, tablets, and computers can suppress melatonin production. Try to avoid screens at least an hour before bedtime or use blue light filtering glasses or apps.

5. Avoid stimulating activities before bedtime - Avoid stimulating activities like exercise, playing video, games, or watching exciting movies at least one hour before bedtime, as they can interfere with our ability to fall asleep.

6. Avoid caffeine and heavy meals close to bedtime - These can disrupt sleep patterns. Try to avoid consuming caffeine in the afternoon and finish eating at least two hours before going to bed.

7. Get some morning sunlight - exposure to sunlight in the morning helps regulate circadian rhythms (physical, mental, and behavioral changes occuring in the body over a 24 - hour cycle), which can help improve sleep quality.

8. Consider keeping a sleep diary - Writing down sleep patterns, including the time to go to bed,

wake up, and factors affecting sleep, can help to identify patterns and make changes to improve the sleep.

Note - It might take some time to notice improvements in sleep quality. Keep patience and don't hesitate to seek professional help if needed.

I. Dr. Deepika Jadhav (77) - A very senior pediatrician with more than 27 years of experience in India and now Director of Ishana Well - Being Center Edgeworth, Newcastle with her own powerful attributes, suggesting to her patients and their caretakers, are given below for the benefit of readers:

1. Look for the positive traits in everyone. Ignore the negative and think of their 1-2 good points to forget and forgive.

2. Treat others with respect as we like to be treated with regard and respect.

3. Don't judge people as we don't know what their journey is. They might be going through a lot of challenges that we might be unaware of.

4. When feeling sad or depressed or even otherwise, count blessings on us. Write a gratitude diary - all the blessings that we have in our life - our mind, our body, our partner, our children, our parents, family, friends, the air we breathe, the food that we eat. there's a lot to be grateful for, that we take for granted.

5. Try to spend the first and the last hour without devices. Inhale fresh air, concentrate on meditation and set goals for the day. Thank

God before sleeping for having a pleasant day counting His blessings again.

6. Spend some time outdoors - go for a walk, play with siblings/ friends / take pet for a walk.

7. Move, move, move - take every opportunity to walk. Park the car / two wheeler farther away from the workplace. Try to have a 15-20 minutes walk after lunch to clear your head, digest food to get more energy for the rest of the day. Climb steps instead of using lift where possible.

8. Have a family dinner on the table at least 2-3 nights a week., when everyone gets to talk about the day - some good and some painful happenings.

9. Limit sugary drinks and processed food to once or twice a week.

10. Do some family activity at least once in a week - going out for a walk, playing board games to connect with children and elderly persons.

11. Hug children while going to school/college, returning home and before sleeping. This gives positive energy to children and youths and they feel secure under the cover of parents. This will create memories for them when they are out of their parents' nest.

12. Teach children to give a helping hand in daily chores to parents- in cooking, cleaning rooms, and in lawn mooing, where possible / kitchen gardening.

13. Have routines and structure in the house. Have limits on devices, not more than one hour a day to school going children, unless needed for home work.
14. Sleep is so important. Have a good bedtime routine. No mobile and no TV in bedrooms.

J. Gauri Shankar (77a) - Senior Manager in Indian Bank in Delhi, India suggests the following attributes based upon his 40 years of experience in the banking sector for readers:

1. Enjoy every moment of life.

2. Real happiness is having good health instead of having a lot of money and a luxurious life.

3. We can enjoy everything if our body is fit.

4. Regular morning and evening walk

5. Self care, Balanced diet and a social circle.

6. Contentment leads to happiness.

7. Respect to all customers / clients leads to success and happiness.

8. Punctuality in office may lead to promotion besides hard work and loyalty to organization

9. Care for parents, grandparents and children makes us happy.

10. Respect to wife and her care makes a healthy and happy family

K. Nitu Gupta (77b) - Senior Principal consultant in Genpact Capital Market, NOIDA and an engineer of repute with a long experience of technology advocates for the following pointers for healthy and happy life:

1. **Cherish the present** - Present is a gift, past can't be done, and future is not in our hands.

2. **Surrounding with positive people** - positive persons will keep building positivity around.

3. **Eat Healthy** - Go for less fried options, buy local fruits and vegetables. Don't order.

4. **Workout 5-6 days a week** - Follow mix workouts, since monotony is boring for the body and the mind.

5. **Practice yoga and meditation** - Very beneficial for bringing positive change in mind and body.**Spend time with family and friends** - They are the first and the ;last base. Take personal time off regularly for fun trips.

6. **Pursue some hobby** - It brings us back to basics and rewires. Keep work and hobby separate.

7. **Journal daily** - It gives space to reflect and do some thinking. It's easier to speak than to pen down feelings in words.

8. **Practice gratitude** - Be grateful for whatever we have and don't have.

9. **Avoid too much social media** - It's an incorrect representation of reality. What's real is not worth sharing many times.

L. Jasbir Kaur, (77c) - The former senior PGT Chemistry in Central School Organization (KVS), Delhi suggests the following attributes for self care and for happiness to others:

1. Going to Gudwara and listening to Gurbani.
2. Supporting education of needy children of maids and relatives by bearing the cost of books, stationery, and school fees.
3. Helping children of the neighborhood in studies at my home free of cost.
4. Taking maids to hospital for treatment and for purchase of medicines.
5. Providing food, biscuits and fruits to children of maids.
6. Visiting old age homes to spend time with inmates and talk to them on my birthday or other such occasions.
7. punctuality, truthfulness and honesty in my day to day activities bless me with happiness.
8. Expressing gratitude to my parents, teachers, children and community members.
9. Appreciating good things and using positive reinforcers to my students in class .
10. Trust in God's will and positive outlook in difficult times.

M. Deepa Gupta (77d) - Mother of two children and a house manager prescribes the following attributes for joyful life and good health:

1. Be friendly with kids to develop confidence and share their feelings with parents.
2. Showing respect to everyone, compassionate and humble for family members and friends, and care of animals and birds.
3. Following disciplined life, and never to insult or make fun of anyone.
4. Regular exercises, yoga and pursuing some hobby of our interest keeps us healthy.
5. Have a jovial atmosphere at home, never compare children with others, and motivate them to improve from their own level.
6. Good intentions and positive thinking help us in remaining joyful and healthy.
7. Developing trust of children, family members, friends and neighbors.
8. Express gratitude to everyone in bundles with politeness.
9. Calling old friends and teachers is the source of positive vibes and happiness.
10. Believe in God and express thankfulness for everything. Self care is the best care.

N. **Ajay Goel (77e)** - A very senior Physician working in a prominent hospital of the beautiful rural community of Rome in New York state for the last 45 years is in itself an ideal doctor, an ideal human being and keeps himself fit by regular meditation and yoga. Dr. Goel shares his following experiences, which may be useful to a common person by amalgamation of body, mind and soul to remain healthy and happy:

1. Eat a low fat diet with high amounts of fruits and vegetables. The diet should also contain enough protein, and low glycemic index food. Following this will cut down the risk of heart disease, diabetes and obesity.

2. Exercise regularly as per suggestion of the physician. This can be as simple as walking, swimming, running or hiking. Exercising regularly increases production of endorphins in the brain which increases sense of well - Being.

3. Do regular exercises like meditation on a regular basis. They stimulate our parasympathetic system and have a calming effect on the mind.

4. Habit of regular reading of newspapers, books and solving riddles, Sudokus also help in sharpening the brain.

5. Soul plays an important role to remain healthy and happy. Treat others as you want to be treated.

6. Be thankful for our good fortune. Pray regularly, which gives comfort in adversity that God is looking out for us and eventual;ly all will be well.

7. Have close relationship with family members, relatives, friends and community members

8. Perform our duties to the best of our ability - in jobs or relationships.
9. Only focus on what is under control. Results will come automatically.
10. Determining what is in and out of control can be challenging at times , but this will come with time and experience.

O. Aryan Gupta (78) - A most creative young boy with exposure of culture of Australian, Asian, American and European continents, Chairman of school in 2022, member of an international fame choral group, student at the University of California, Berkeley now and at present enjoying the culture of Spain at University of Barcelona suggests following attributes to remain healthy and happy from his perspective:

1. Find positive outlets for stress (working out, journaling, meditation, music)
2. Be innovative and create
3. Surround yourself with people that encourage growth
4. Be curious and not judgmental (always ask questions and have a passion for learning; don't be close minded)
5. Don't compare yourself to others, rather understand what they are doing differently
6. Be kind to **everyone**
7. Appreciate differences in one another

8. Begin every task with a goal in mind. A clear direction in one's work is crucial for producing timely outcomes

9. Try everything. Live life with no regrets

10. Don't listen to any of the aforementioned points. There's no point in memorizing this advice because happiness and joy comes from within, and you will know where to find it.

P. Bharat Gupta (77f), Director, Resilience Risk of HSBC Innovation Bank, London A renowned with a long experience of more than 25 years with his clients feels that the following pointers can help readers to enjoy a joyful and healthy life :

1. Get proper sleep, number of hours depending upon the age.

2. Stay active with 3-4 hours of exercise during the week.

3. We should take care of mental health along with our physical health.

4. Spend time outdoors away from the media.

5. Monitor and control social media usage. Never feel pressured to be on all social media channels or respond to all messages straight away.

6. Have fiends and be part of community groups.

7. Involve self in charitable activities. Helping and giving gives more pleasure than earning.

8. Do financial planning from an early age. Financial stability is important for mental health.

9. Never compare yourself with others. Compare with yourself only for vertical mobility.

10. Keep learning and bremain selfish to spend time on our own interest. Self care makes one healthy and happy.

Q. Naren Goel (77g) - A very senior financial analyzer, CFO of many MNCs of America and at present CFO of IPS at San Diego is a very widely read and widely traveled big business magnet. Naren is very sober and always very eager to help his acquaintances has agreed to share his views about Joyful and healthy living, with a personal physical trainer for his good health. The following suggestions by Naren may be helpful for the readers :

1. While doing something for others, never expect in return, to avoid disappointment.

2. Enjoy your duty- it can be our own work, things we do for children,family and friends, but without expectations.

3. Let's keep ourselves active - both physically and mentally. Can we push ourselves to do more than we think?

4. Be kind to people, especially involved in doing menial jobs. Help them and guide them to do better.

5. Get involved in charitable events that allow us to help people in need.

6. Let's be aware of what we are. Never act like someone else. Some people are introverted, and some are extroverted. Sometimes introverted persons try to be extroverted due to societal pressure, but not for good health and happiness.

7. Being competitive can be good, but don't make it an obsession. Otherwise, we become jealous of others' achievement, trying to pressure ourselves in an unhealthy way.

8. Keep a balance between day to day activities.

9. Respect our partner to lead a happy life.

10. We may try to be a good listener, since silence is gold.

R. Rashmi Goel (77h), - An Oncology Specialist and a senior researcher at Merck at L. A. in the U.S.A. is a friend of friends, meeting people with a smile is very popular in her community. Based upon her global exposure, Rashmi opines for the following as the most important pointers to remain healthy and happy:

1. Happiness and wellness starts inside us. We don't need anyone to tell us what happiness is. Our happiness is about us and what we value in our daily life.

2. Love yourself the way we are. Nobody is perfect in this world. We admire each other for certain things. Dwell on those rather than the negatives.

3. Self care - taking care of us should always be the first priority. Only then can we take care of people around us.
4. Stop caring about what others think of us. It doesn't bring joy or happiness.
5. Living in the moment and enjoying the moment, and staying focused on the moment should be the right approach to life.
6. Treating others as we like to be treated should be the gurumantra to keep people happy.
7. Kindness towards everyone brings kindness back to us.
8. Always remain grateful instead of always asking for more.
9. Giving - giving is the best way of feeling fulfilled. Always follow this.
10. Enjoy the process , not the outcome happening our way.
11. Do what makes us happy. Work out, if you feel better, enjoy walks looking around on beautiful trees. leaves, flowers, people and traffic. Connect with people.

S. Preeti Gupta (77i) - A Senior lecturer in Physics in Hindu Vidyapeeth Sr. Secondary School, Sonipat with more than 20 years of teaching experience suggests the following attributes for students to remain healthy and happy:

1. **Balanced Routine -** Encouraging students to balance academics, extracurricular activities

and rest, which helps reduce stress and promotes overall well - being.

2. **Physical Activity** - Regular exercise or participation in sports, which is vital for both physical and mental health.

3. **Positive Relationships** - Fostering a sense of belonging and meaningful friendships. Teacherscan encourage teamwork and respectful communication among students.

4. **Healthy Eating Habits -** Guiding students to make informed choices about nutrition and the importance of eating balanced meals.

5. **Emotional Resilience** - Helping students develop coping mechanisms to handle challenges, stress, and failures with a positive mindset.

6. **Creativity and Hobbies-** Supporting students in exploring their interests outside academics, such as art, music, painting or any other hobby that brings joy.

7. **Sleep Hygiene** - Emphasizing the importance of adequate sleep to improve focus, mood, and learning.

8. **Mindfulness and Mental Well** - Being - Encouraging practices like mindfulness, meditation, or relaxation techniques to manage anxiety and stay grounded.

9. **Time Management Skills** - Teaching students to prioritize and manage their time effectively,

allowing them to balance work and play without feeling overburdened.

10. **Self - Reflection and Gratitude** - Encouraging students to practice gratitude, reflect on their achievements, and focus on personal growth rather than competition with peers.

The above attributes help students lead fulfilling, healthy lives, both inside and outside the classroom and others when integrated in our life, can help to create a harmonious balance and lead to a joyful and healthy existence. What should we think contributes most to our sense of well- being? Discipline of punctuality, regular exercise, and the above attributes for self-care are the traits leading to internal happiness and good health but real happiness is attained life long by taking care of others as discussed above.

CHAPTER – 15
PHILANTHROPY & ANECDOTES OF INTERNAL HAPPINESS

There are thousands of people all over the globe doing charity for the needy persons from their corporate funds as policy of their companies and also for their happiness and well- being of family members and their employees. Jamshedji Nusserwanji Tata (97) born on March 3, 1839 was an Indian industrialist and philanthropist, who founded the Tata Group, India's biggest conglomerate company in 19TH century and established the city of Jamshedpur, before his passing away on May 1,1904. He was the biggest donor of the 19th century. His donations were recognized posthumously, being ranked first in the "Hurun Philanthropists of the century (2021)" by total donations of US $102 billion (in 2021 Prices). As of February 2024, some of the top philanthropists include billionaires (98) who have donated large amounts of money to various causes. Warren Buffett is the biggest giver for the fourth year in a row, with US $56.7 billion in lifetime. Bill Gates and Melinda French Gates stand at position number two by donating US$42.5 billion over their lifetime, and George Soros occupies 3rd position by donating US $21 billion in 2024.

Warren Buffett (99) born on August 30, 1930 at Omaha, Nebraska, U.S. did his BS from University of Pennsylvania and MS from Columbia University.

Buffett is an American businessman, investor, and philanthropist who currently serves as chairman and CEO of Berkshire Hathaway. As a result of his investment success, Buffett is one of the best- known investors in the world. As of June 2024, he had a net worth of US $135 billion, making him the tenth-richest person in the world.

Bill Gates (46, 100) born on October 28, 1955 in Seattle, Washington is an American businessman known for the creation of Microsoft and his charity work across the globe. Developing a strong interest in computing during his adolescence, he later dropped out of Harvard to found Microsoft with his friend Paul Allen. As of 2021, he was the third richest person in the United States with a net worth of over US $124 billion. Gates earned the majority of his wealth from Microsoft. He has been instrumental in Covid-19 reliefs with the donation of US $1.75 billion for the production of medical supplies and distribution. Gates is often routed as the epitome of self- made success and he is looked upon favorably throughout the world due to his humanitarian work. Melinda French Gates (46,101), born on August 15, 1964 is an American philanthropist, businesswoman, and advocate for women and girls. She is the co-chair of Bill Melinda Foundation. She is the owner of multimedia product developer and manager at Microsoft, and the ex-wife of its co-founder and billionaire Bill Gates. French Gates has consistently ranked as one of the world's most powerful women by Forbes magazine, in 2000. She and her then-husband Bill Gates co-founded the Bill & Melinda Gates Foundation, the world's largest private charitable organization. She and her ex-husband have been awarded the US Presidential Medal of Freedom and the French Legion of Honor. In early May, 2021, Bill and Melinda Gates announced their divorce. Melinda was recognized as one of the BBC's 100 women of 2021. Melinda owns a net worth of US$10.5 billion as in 2024.

George Soros (99) born on August 12, 1930 in Budapest in Hungary is a Hungarian - American businessman, investor, and Philanthropist. At the early age of 17 years he shifted to the United Kingdom in 1947. He got B.Sc. in philosophy in 1951 from London School of Economics and then a Master of Science in 1954. He is a Holocaust survivor and a billionaire. As of October 2023, he had a net worth of US$6.7 billion, whereas his net worth in 2011 was estimated as US$25 billion. Forbes magazine called Soros the "Most Generous Giver" in terms of percentage of his net worth. He is a resident of New York now.

According to The Edel Give Hurun India Philanthropy list 2023, the top four Indian philanthropists are – Shiv Nadar and family, who donated INR 2,042 crore through HCL Technologies for arts, culture, and heritage, Azim Premji and family, who donated INR 1,774, crores, Mukesh Ambani and Family, who donated INR 411 crores in 2022, most of which went to the cause of education, followed by Kumar Manglam Birla and Family with donation of INR 285 crores in the field of education and other areas.

Shiv Nadar (104), born on 14 July, 1945 is an Indian billionaire industrialist and philanthropist. He was the founder and chairman of HCL Technologies set up in 1976, and is chairman of the Shiv Nadar Foundation. Since the mid 1990s, he has focused his efforts on developing the educational system of India through the Shiv Nadar Foundation. According to Firbes, Nadar has an estimated net worth of US$40 billion as of August, 2024.

Azim Hashim Prem ji (105) born on 24 July 1945 is an Indian businessman and a philanthropist, and the chairman of Wipro Limited. Premji remains a non-executive member of the board and founder chairman. According to the Forbes Bloomberg Billionaires Index, Premji's net worth is estimated at US $25 billion in 2023. In 2013, he agreed to give away at least half of his wealth by signing the giving pledge. Premji started with a US $2.2 billion donation to the Azim Premji Foundation, focused on education in India.

Mukesh Ambani (106), one of the richest people in the world is also a big philanthropist who founded the Reliance Foundation. He is the managing director and chairman of Reliance Industries, is the most opulent businessman, and is known worldwide for the marriage of his youngest son, Anant with Radha, where he spent many thousands of crores of rupees in the wedding for the happiness of his children and the guests. Bill Gates, Mark Zuckerberg, Prime Minister of India and thousands of people from India and abroad were the invitees. The most important was Mukesh's inner will of hosting lunch/ dinner for 60, 000 residents of his village and surrounding areas of Jamnagar district of Gujarat to give a good feel of delicacies served by the Ambani group on the very special occasion of the family. This was the real charity for all people of those villages to take blessings of all residents and especially the elder members of the community for Anant and Radha.

Kumar Manglam Birla, the chairman of the Aditya Birla group donated Rs. 242 crores in the field of education and other charities all over India. Birla temples are found in big cities of India. When in Delhi, visit to Birla temple with family members was a regular feature to have darshan of Hindu deities in the temple. After coming to Bhopal. We used to pay a visit on weekends to the Laxmi Narain temple made by Birlas on the Jail road of Bhopal. Birla group has a very old history with association of G.D. Birla (107) with Gandhi JI since 1916 during India's freedom struggle. After India's independence on 15, August 1947, G.D,Birla took big steps towards making our nation self-reliant by setting up Grasim company just after 10 days, and then Hindalco, our metal flagship. To the great surprise of the readers, G. D. Birla had donated a huge amount to Aligarh Muslim University and also helped in setting up Banaras Hindu University (BHU). He raised several temples, planetariums and hospitals across India. Under Aditya Vikram Birla's leadership, the group became a global leader in viscose staple fiber production, palm oil refining, insulators, and carbon black.

Goodness and kindness never go unrewarded. We find temples and hospitals in big cities, where thousands of devotees visit Birla temples in the early morning and evening to pray for welfare of their family members and also wish good luck for Birlas, who developed such beautiful temples in their city. I know one such hospital at Indore in the name of "Bombay Hospital Indore" where the consulting fee for any outdoor patients is Rs.1600, but the hospital has a special facility for poor people who can have access to the tertiary hospital by paying only Rs. 10 and get free consultation from the super specialists and treatment also under the special category. Same facility is provided by other tertiary hospitals of Birla group throughout India.

KBC (Kaun Banega Crorepati) program conducted by Amitabh Bachhan (108), super hero of 20th century India on Sony channel is very popular, where Amitabh Bacchan asks questions to persons coming on the hot seat and the participant can earn up to Rs. One crore by answering 15 questions correctly and seven crores by giving correct answers of 16th question. The program started in 2001 is held almost every year. In the present series (2024), Birla group has announced free education of as many children based upon questions asked by Amitabh Bachhan during a particular session of the show. By now (Oct., 2024), the number has crossed 950, meaning thereby that the group will bear all expenses of 950 or more children's education from the next academic session or this session only.

Many trusts of Tata group (109) are extending exemplary philanthropic services to mankind in India and abroad. Sir Ratan Tata Trust established in 1919 is one of the oldest philanthropic institutions in India, and has played a pioneering role in changing traditional ideas of charity. The Navajbai Ratan Tata Trust , founded in memory of Sir Ratan Ttata's wife in 1974 works together with the Sir Ratan Tata trust to bestow grants. Tata Education and Development Trust set up in September 2008, promotes social welfare with considerable importance on national development. Bai Hirabai J.N. Navsari Charitable Institution established on December 7, 1923 has the same Board of Trustees as that of Sir Ratan Tata Trust. The Sarvajanik Seva Trust, registered as a public charitable trust in 1975 provides grants to individuals for reimbursing costs incurred towards medical treatment, besides giving grants/scholarships to deserving students to pursue higher studies in India.

The Tata group has a history of philanthropy for the last one century that includes supporting education, healthcare and other causes before and after independence of India. The trust established India's first cancer care hospital in Bombay (now Mumbai), and have seeded and supported several leading institutions- including amongst others, the Tata Center for Technology and Design at Indian Institute of Technology Bombay (IIT-B), the Tata Center for Technology and Design within the Massachusetts institute of Technology (MIT). According to the EdelGive Foundation and Hurun Report 2021, the Tata group, Jamsetji Tata, has been recognized as the most charitable person of the past century, having donated a staggering Rs. 829,734 crore. Ratan Tata the visionary businessman with ethics, credibility, transparency, a great brand of India in many sectors and Chairman of Tata Group heaved his last breath on the night of 9 october, 2024 during the most auspicious period of Navratri at Bombay. A great loss to India and the world where his many companies were serving citizens of 121 countries. May the noble soul of Ratan Tata rest in peace. Om Shanti, Om!

The above list of international fame philanthropists of India and abroad is of those who have donated billions of dollars in charity to uplift the living standard of weaker sections of the society, but there are millions of middle class men and women around us, who have been constantly busy in bringing cheers on the faces of needy persons. In the good old days, the well to do families used to help the community members by opening common places called Dharamshalas or inns for the stay of travelers, for organizing family functions like marriage of their children or meeting points of village / city elderly persons. These places were also used for organizing any religious function during the festival season. I remember that there were two such concrete buildings called Chaupal in my village even 70 years ago. If some made arrangements for potable water by digging wells, and fitting hand pumps, the others provided shade as the resting place for village elderly persons and their animals by planting bunches of trees with water facility. Some opened schools and colleges without looking towards the government, and a few individuals or groups of community members developed temples/mosques/churches/ Gurdwaras. In my own town, I got school and college education run by private management, charging a very nominal fee but providing all facilities of neat and clean classrooms with provision of fans, comfortable benches and desks for students and cemented black boards and drinking water facility, and above all the excellent teaching faculty. Those charities and facilities were no less than offered by millionaires or billionaires in big cosmopolitan cities. Thousands of boys and girls like me got almost free education by studying in such privately managed schools and colleges. This is the debt on us of those philanthropists. We should now contribute in a better way by helping our alma maters. Readers may be aware of such many contributors in their community who are helping the weaker sections of the society to bring happiness to themselves and others.

There are many persons in our society, who regularly visit hospitals to help attendants of patients coming from faraway places for distribution of food packets and fruits daily or on weekends as per their convenience. By doing so they get satisfaction and inner happiness for themselves as well as for others. All countries have their own traditions of caring for others. Hindus can boast of a large number of religious festivals being celebrated throughout the year. Navratri festivals are celebrated during April and October for 9-10 days. During these periods people observe fasts for Goddess Durga and there is tradition of feeding girls below 10 years of age on the 8th or 9th day of the celebration. The girls of all communities are put in high esteem, and worship is done thinking them as representatives of Goddess Durga. This is almost common throughout India to pay respect to the fair sex, but some mishappenings are reported from some part of the country which is a matter of great concern for the society. Bhandaras (free community lunch or dinner) are also very common these days. During our visits to Vaishno Devi in northern India, we always came across many such Bhandaras run by different businesspersons from different parts of the country in honor of the Goddess to take her blessings by feeding the devotees walking to the shrine for worship and blessings of their deity.

Gurdwaras are such holy places run by volunteers of Sikh community where Langar (free food consisting of bread, vegetables, tea, water and sometimes sweet also) is served to all devotees after having darshan of Guru Granth Saheb and Guru Nanak Dev Ji, founder of Sikhism in 15th century. Such charity and service to society is rarely observed in the world. Sikhs are the persons putting turban on their head and following principles of Sikhism as prescribed by Guru Nanak and other Gurus. They are very hard working people, honest, God fearing, friends of friends, most reliable, fearless and warriors, and constantly contributing a part of their earnings to Gurdwaras in their neighborhood. We have been visiting Gurdwaras in our town since our childhood and always feel happy, content and full of positive energy after visiting Gurudwaras.

We also got a chance to visit Gurudwara in the mid night in Joshi math (uttarakhand) during our visit to Badrinath in 1986, where we were served hot tea and woolen beddings for the chilly night free of coast. Such a humanitarian gesture is rarely observed in any part of the world. We also got chances to visit Gurdwaras at San Jose in America with Bobby, Shuchita, Kunal and Aryan in 2015 and in Australia while going from Newcastle to Gold Coast with Dolly, Vineet, Anshul and Ishana in 2018. Every time we got the same feeling of inner happiness and contentment after having darshan of Guru Granth Saheb and Guru Nanak Ji, followed by taking Prasadam of Langar.

Many temples in India and in foreign countries also run the facility of Prasadam after darshan of Hindu deities. San Jose Temple in California is very popular among Hindus as there are beautiful marble idols of all deities in the temple. Devotees from different parts of India are living at San Jose for the last many years have developed the San Jose Hindu Vedic Temple by donating thousands and thousands of dollars of their earnings. Whenever we visit our children in America, they always take us to that temple and we always feel very lucky to have darshan of all deities followed by Prasadam. Temple at Livermore is also having a very high following of devotees of Southern India. The temple has an eye-catching structure with lush green lawns. Prasadam is the essential feature of all Hindu temples. This is also a great service to the community by some philanthropists by raising such beautiful temples for the community members, where they can worship and meditate for satisfaction of mind, contentment of soul and inner happiness of mind and body. We should also contribute as per our will, whenever we visit such places as a good gesture towards community members or the needy persons.

D. Prakash Rao (110), aged 60, runs a school- "Asha Assawsana" just beside the boundary wall of Samaj Press in Buxi Bazar area in cuttack for 70 underprivileged children free of cost. Rao, who started the school 14 years back, is managing it with 50 % of income from his tea stall only. Such a highly devoted person, who has donated blood 205 times since 1976 till now. This is just one example in the society but there are thousands and thousands of people living in almost every part of India and many other countries as well to make this planet the most enjoyable place to live in by keeping others happy. But God is great and He always takes care of such people. They are always blessed with good health and happiness.

Diversity is beauty, which is observed everywhere and around us. Either we can remain happy by enjoying this diversity like five fingers of our hand, where each finger has a different role to play, or we may curse ourselves by finding ourselves at a very low level in comparison to others. Comparison and competition lead to tension, jealousy, frustration, unhappiness and ultimately poor mental and physical health. By following generosity of billionaires, millionaires or middle class or lower class persons like Mr. Rao, who makes his two times meals by running a tea stall but spending 50 percent of his earning to run a school of more than 50 children by donating 50 percent of his family income, we can think of helping others. There was a time in most of our lives when a single dollar /rupee meant a lot for us, but now if we have thousand rupees or hundred dollars in our wallet, can't we spare, one tenth of our wealth to bring shine on the needy persons by helping them in our own ways, without comparing with anyone.

CHAPTER -16
WHAT WE CAN DO FOR JOYFUL AND HEALTHY LIVING

We can adopt a few of the following points in our life to remain Joyful and Happy Living:

1. Get up before Sunrise and express thanks to God for everything we have.
2. Switch on the light, roll the bedding, open the door for fresh air and walk a few steps.
3. Drink one or two glasses of luke warm water sip by sip while sitting. Keep hydrated by drinking at least 2.5 liters of water daily.
4. Start meditation, have deep breathing and do a few simple stretching exercises.
5. Prepare one, two or more cups of tea depending upon family members after brushing and easing out.
6. Start reading the newspaper to keep abreast with happenings in the world.
7. Go out for the morning walk in the nearby park or garden or in our own campus. Can also drive to the distant park and then have a walk at least for 40 minutes. A 30 minute evening walk is also equally useful. While walking, we should make movements of our hands too to keep us active.
8. Take a body massage with mustard or any other oil of your own choice and take a shower while sitting or standing depending upon the age. If you

JOYFUL AND HEALTHY LIVING

are sixty plus, you must use rubber mats in the bathroom.

9. Do worship of any God or Sub God for the welfare of self, family members, relatives, friends and community members.
2. Take breakfast of choice, but better to have light breakfast with a glass of milk. Curd may be taken during lunch with pulses and vegetables.
3. Help the spouse in kitchen work as far as possible to keep the partner happy.
4. Go out to meet community members and do some social service for the community.
5. Check messages, reply and talk at least to two or three family members, friends or relatives to know about their welfare. Read some interesting books and watch the TV channel of choice.
6. Help the spouse in kitchen work by cutting vegetables, or as per desire of the spouse. Respect for each other makes life happy and enjoyable.
7. Never argue with the spouse. Even if he/she is wrong, keep calm, but tell later by pointing out mistakes. If both partners argue and start crying, that will lead to quarrel and fighting. Always avoid fighting with your wife as the wife is always right. Follow this principle with family members, relatives and friends.
8. Give flowers to your spouse to keep him/her in good humor.
9. Never forget the birthday of the spouse and marriage anniversary and also bring some gifts.

10. Kindness is a great virtue. Be kind to all to remain healthy and happy.
11. Inculcate the habit of forgetting and forgiving. Get rid of the revengeful attitude to avoid tension and spoiling your health unnecessarily.
12. When you feel like losing your temper, start counting up to 20 and have a glass of water to calm down. Losing our temper increases our B.P. which is detrimental to our health.
13. Keep visiting family members, relatives and friends to enquire about their welfare.
14. Spare time to visit places of your religious bent of mind or heritages.
15. Develop the habit of respecting all religions and their customs as all religions preach for life values of love to all, honesty, punctuality, sincerity to work and life skills.
16. Always offer a glass of water to workers /maids working at our place. A cup of tea with snacks sometimes will make them very loyal to us.
17. Offer a piece of cake to maids on special occasions like birthdays, marriage anniversaries and also give them some money for sweets to their children.
18. Always take care of workers of your society by helping them by materials or cash as per their need. Always give them proper love and respect. They will be very helpful to us in our time of need.
19. Security guards of our campus are the most important people. They also deserve care and respect. Keep helping them with petty things,

which they value the most, but never give money as a loan.
20. Never boast of property or own wealth to make others zealous.
21. Be a good listener, since silence is Gold.
22. Good narration is bliss but don't keep talking for too long, which distracts the attention of listeners/ peers.
23. Keep screening old books, clothes and domestic items and distribute them to needy ones.
24. Save water by offering half glass of water to guests, using a small tumbler while saving and brushing and keep the water tap open to the minimum to avoid wastage of water. Must ensure that the foot valve of the overhead tank is not broken. If so, change it immediately to check overflow of water.
25. Save energy by switching off fans and tube lights of the unoccupied rooms. Avoid minimum use of air conditioners as they are main sources of global warming. This will save our energy bill as well as the energy to be used by other needy ones.
26. Take care of the environment. Don't concretize the whole front yard or backyard. Keep space for planting trees, flowers and passage for water flow to increase the underground water level.
27. Avoid making high pitch noise, detrimental for health. Take care of your neighbors.
28. Use minimum honks while driving vehicles. Don't try to overtake others' vehicles.
29. Must take care of our own vehicles by regular servicing and checking of noise pollution.

30. May join some music, dance or painting class as per our interest and facilities.
31. Most of us live alone after retirement and settle children at their own places. Our neighbors are our best friends and well wishers. Have good relations with them. Try to adjust without remembering the past, as adjustment is life. Contentment is a real source of happiness. Have at least 3- 4 mobile numbers of neighbors or friends.
32. We should be thankful to God, even if we have one real friend.
33. Don't expect anything from anyone. Keep giving instead of taking.
34. Avoid backbiting, which results in spoiling personal relationships.
35. We may have dinner at least two hours before sleeping. Better to have a light dinner. Most followers of the Jain religion don't eat anything after Sunset. We may follow this useful habit to keep us healthy.
36. We must have a few big laughs during the day to keep our lungs healthy.
37. We may start writing a daily diary to express ourselves and to make note of daily happenings.
38. We may switch off the TV at least one hour before going to bed.
39. We may express our gratitude to people who helped us during the day and to God before going to bed.

40. Develop the habit of regular gratitude / thanksgiving like Americans.
41. While sleeping, we may sleep with our right side touching the bed and worshiping God.
42. Pray to God for a better tomorrow and have a sound sleep with good dreams.
43. elderly persons may take special precautions while getting up by moving their legs in opposite directions for 1-2 minutes, before touching the floor and remaining as such in the sitting position for one minute. They may not do any exercise in the bathroom. also avoid doing strenuous exercises on an empty stomach.

Many more such attributes we may include in our daily life based upon our own experiences and experiences of our elders, family members, friends and relatives. Life may be taken as a circle made up of many small slices, out of which many of us might have enjoyed during our good days on different family functions or on our achievements, but some may be full of agony and distress. We should take those days with patience and keep struggling without giving up.

REFERENCES

1. Google, World Economy of top 10 Countries by IMF, March 2024.
2. Jennifer De Paola, Happiness Researcher, University of Helsinki, Times of India, p.8, Bhopal India, 21 March 2024.
3. Vitamin D, Google, https://www.healthline.com> vita..., 4 April 2023.
4. Photosynthesis, Hans Lambers, James Alan Bassham, The Editors of Encyclopedia Britannica, last updated 1 Marc , 2024.
5. NCERT, Science Textbook for class X, New Delhi, India, p.96, 2006.
6. E.W. Uvarov &D.R.Chapman, ELBS & Penguin Books, p. 292, 1943.
7. Slavery U.S. vs Europe, Gemini, March 2024
8. Martin Luther King Jr. Gemini, https://e.vwikipedia.org/wiki/Wikipedia.
9. Aaron Bushenel, U.S. Army man, Air Force, Washington D.C. Times of India, p. 2, 27 Feb. 2024.
10. Navalny, Times of India, p.2. 27 Feb. 2024.
10 A. Nirmla Gupta, Brahmakumari since 1965, RG Tower, B 2103, NOIDA, Sector 120, Uttar Pradesh, India.
11. Adam Grant Think Again : The Power of Knowing What you don't Know, Viking, pp. 1-320, Feb. 2021.

12. Steve Jobs, Google, https://abcnews.go.com>story, 15 August,2011.
13. Warren Buffett, CEO Berkshire Hathway, Sailicionindia, 2024.
14. Vashudhaiva Kutumbkam,Sanskrit Phrase from Maha Upanishad, https://www.uaf,edu>news>Friday, 9Sep. 2023.
15. Rigveda, Welfare of All, https://www,goodreads.com,1500 BCE.
16. Ramcharit Manas, Shrimad Goswami Tulsidas,Geeta Press Gorakhpur -273005, pp. 1-975, 2012.
17. Bhagwat Geeta, Rupesh Thakur Prakasan, Kachori street, Varanasi, pp. 1-240, 2004.
18. Fight of Mahabharat, October- November, 900 BCE, https://www.hindustantimrs .com >...
19. King Harishchandra,Google, https://hinduism.stackexchange.com >...
20. Harishchandra as chandel, Google,https://www.vedantu.com > stories
21. Literacy in India in 2023, Google,https:??cyboard school.com > ways...
22. Population of India In 2024, Google,https://www.worldometers.info. > i...
23. infrastructureWikipedia:https://en.wikipedia.org > wiki> i...

    Vandebharat, Google,https://www.jagranjosh.com, list _of_

25. Passengers traveling by air, Google,https://skift.com. 15 April 2024.
26. Happy cities of India,Google,https://www.timesnownews.com> 28 October 2020.
27. India at Olympics,https://en.wikipedia.org > wiki > i...
28. Cricket World cup 1983 Final, youtube channel,https://www.icc-cricket.com.
29. Chankya,Google.https://en.wikipedia.org > wiki...
30. Dhananand, https://en.wikipedia.org/wiki.
31. Socrates, Google,https://www.masterclass.com
32. Nicolaus Copernicus,Google,https://www.pas.rochester.edu>c ...
33. Galileo galilei, Google, https://www.pbslearningmedia.org .> ...
34. Isaac Newton, Google, https://earthobservatory.nasa.gov > ...
35. Rabindranath Tagore,Wikipedia, .org > wiki >R...
36. C.V. Raman, https://en.wikipedia.org/wiki/C_V_Raman.
37. Joshimath landslide,Google,https://www.neindianexpress.com 6 May 2024.
38. Silkyara tunnel tragedy,Google,https://www.Wikipedia.org > wiki > U...

39. CO2re;leased by an AC, https :// www.ajer.org > papers...ajer.org, 5 Feb. 2023.
40. Greenhouse Gas Emissions, Google,https :// www.epa.gov >green ... U.S. Environmental Protection agency, Aug. 2023.
41. Deforestation, ArabellaRuiz, Google, https:// the roundup.org. en-us , the Nature Conservancy, 18 November,2023.
42. Bawadies of Rajasthan, https://en.wikipedia.org >wiki...
43. Roof – water Harvesting System of Mandu Fort, https:// files. cluster 2.hostgator.co.in, 30 May, 2014.
44. Use of electricity in dishwashers in U.S.A. ,Google, https://www. Inspireacleanenergy.com >...
45. Population of India, households using dishwashers, https://www.worldometers. Info > i..., 27 June, 2024.
46. Bill Gate,Google, https:// www. Gates foundation. Org >...$ national medals.org > laureate.
47. Mark Zukerberg, Google, https:// pres.farm > mark-Zukerberg... 6 June, 2024.
48. Tesla, Google, https:// www.hertz.com > blog W...
49. Electric Vehicles, Robert Anderson, Google,https:// en.wikipedia. org > wiki.
50. Electric Bus, Scania- Vabis (1940),https"//www.scania.com >heritage.

51. Sydney Harbor sudden rise. https://www.australiancruisegroup.com.au >... 17,000 years ago.
52. Darling Harbor, google,https://nbglandscapes.com.au > his, 1988.
53. Opera House, Google.https://www.https://en.wikipedia.org > wiki >s...
54. Sydney Harbor Bridge,Google, https://www.britannica.com > topic, 14 June 2024.
55. Chandigarh, Google,https://www.chandigarh,gov.in >...
56. Kasha Viswanath, Wikipedia,https://en.wikipedia.org > wiki.
57. Vishwanath temple by Vkrmaditya, study.com.https:// study.com > lesson > his.... 17 March,2023.
58. Niagara Falls history, https://www.niagarafallsstatepark.com >...
59. Indian States, google,https:// byjus.com > Social Science, 2024.
60. Indian Languages, https://en.wikipedia.org. > wiki >L... census, 2001
61. Amarnathyatra,https://www.kestral.aviation.com > 17, Jan. 2024.
62. Vaishno Devi Temple – Wikipedia,https://en.wikipedia.org > wiki.
63. Visitors to Vaisho Devi in 2023, Google, Statista,https://www.statista.com > stat.., 19 June, 2024.

64. Arushi India, https://www.arushi – india.org 1989.
65. On happiness and human potentials: a review of research on hedonic and eudaimonic approach, R.M. Ryan et.al. Annu Rev Psychol, 2001.
66. Tansen, Google, https://www.britanica.com >Tan... 27 May, 2024.
67. Ameen Sayani, Google, https://m.economictimes.com > arti, 21 Feb. 2021.
68. Binaca Geetmala, Google, https://m.economic times.com>art.
69. ED. Sheren, Google, https:// times of India.indiatimes.com>... 13 May 2024.
70. Michael Jackson, https://en.m.wikipedia,org/wiki/ Michael Jackson.
71. Usha Gupta, Classical Singer, Flamingo , Aakriti Eco City, Bhopal-462039, India since Nov. 2010.
72. Vineet Jadhav, G.P. Edgeworth Family Practice, Newcastle, Australia, since July, 2007.
73. Nupur Ghosh, Music Center For All Ages, Flamingo , Bhopal -462039, India, since 2011.
74. Bobby Gupta, Software Engineer, Silicon Valley, America, since June 2014.
75. Shuchita Gupta, CTO, Global Health Care, IBM, Silicon Valley, America, since June 2014.
76. Kavita Gupta Ghdale, Bombay Hospital , Indore- 4502010, India, since Jan. 2020.

77. Deepika Jadhav, John Hunter Hospital & now Director, Ishana Well – Being Center, Edgeworth, Newcastle, since July 2007.

77 a. Gauri Shankar, Sr. Manager, Indian Bank, New Delhi, since 1985.

77 b. Nitu Gupta, Sr. Principal Consultant, Genpact Headstrong, NOIDA , since 2007

77 c. Jasbir Kaur, Sr. PGT(Chemistry), Central Schools KVS (retd), New Delhi.

77 d. Deepa Gupta, B.Sc. B.Ed. (RCE Bhopal NCERT), House Manager, Pune.

77 e. Ajay Goel, Physician, Rome Hospital , 6780 Stokes Westernville, AVA,, Rome, 13303, US.A. since 1988.

77 f. Bharat Gupta, Director, Resilience Risk, HSBC Innovation Bank London.

77 g. Naren Goel, CFO, IPS, San Diego, L.A., U.S.A

77 h. Rashmi Goel, Oncology Specialist, Merck, L.A., U.S.A. Orange County,

77 i. Preeti Gupta, Senior Lecturer in Physics, Hindu Vidyapeeth Sr. Secondary school, Sonipat.

78. Aryan Gupta, B.S. (UCB) and member of Choir Group, silicon Valley, America, since July, 2014,

79. P. T. Narsimhan, IIT Kanpur, Google, https://www.iitk.ac.in > P...

80. Birju Maharaj, Googlepedia, https://en.wikipedia.org >wiki >...

81. Mrinalini Sarabhai, Google, Wikipedia, https:// Wikipedia. Org >wiki.
82. Rukumani Devi Arundale, Google, Wikipedia, https:// en.m. Wikipedia.org/wiki/Rukmini_Devi_Arundale.
83. Padma Subramanya, Google, Wikipedia, https:// en.m. Wikipedia, https:// en.m. Wikipedia.org / wiki, main_ Page.
84. Yamii Krishnamurthy, Google, Wikipedia, https:// en.m.wikipedia,org/wiki Yaamini _ Krishnamurthy.
85. Sonal Mansingh, Google, https:// www. Sohamasmi.org> gur…
86. Michael Jackson, largest attendance, https://www.quora.com .What-w…10 Feb, 2016.
87. Nupur Music Concert, E Square, stop no 12, Bhopal-462016, India, 27 April, 2024.
88. S.P. Sharma, Reader in Physics, RIE<Bhopal (retd), March 2006.
89. Teejan Bai, Pandavani, https:// www.onmanorma.com >… 13 May. 2019.
90. Bharat Bhavan, Google, https:// bharatbhavan.org, 13 Feb. 1982.
91. Vasu Jadhav, a renowned artist, Jadhav's Farmhouse, village Amoli, Bhopal, since 2001.
92. Leonardo Da Vainci, Vincent Van Gogh, weloveart.com, https:// www.weloveart.com >… 16 Sep. 2023.
93. Pablo Picaso, Google, Wikipedia, https:// en.m.wikipedia.org /wiki/ Pablo_ Picaso.

94. Sahu R.M. , 10 Golden Rules for Seniors for happiness, Flamingo 178, Aakriti Eco City, Bhopal – 462039, India, August, 2024
95. Anand Chandeliya, Attributes to lead Happy Post –Retired Life as suggested by Prof. Tripathi of B.H.U., Flamingo 242, Aakriti Eco City, Bhopal-462039, India, Aug. 2024.
96. Mukesh Sahni, Improving Sleep Quality, Flamingo 147, Aakriti Eco City, Bhopal-462039, India.
97. Jamshedji Tata, Google, https:// en.Wikipedia.org > wiki > Ja.
98. Top three Global Philanthropists in 2024, AI overview, Feb. 2024.
99. Warren Buffet, https://en.m.wikipedia, org/wiki/Warren Buffet, June 2024.
100. Bill Gates, https:// study.com >lesson > bill-g...
101. Melinda French Gates,https"//en. m. Wikipedia . org/ wiki / Melinda _ French_Gates, May 2021,2024.
102. George Soros, Wikipedia, https:// en .m. Wikipedia . org /wiki / George_ Soros, 2011,2023, 2024.
103. Edel Hurun, Indian Philanthropists, Google, 2023, August 2024.
104. Shiv Nadar's Path to Philanthropy, Fortune India, Retrieved, 22 Feb. 2023.
105. Azim Premji, Encyclopedia, Britannica. Retrieved, 10 August 2021.

106. Mukesh Ambani, https:// faster capital.com. 18 June 2024.
107. G.D. Birla, https: // www.aditya bilrla.com
108. Amitabh Bacchan, superstar of 20th century and organizer of Kaun Banega Crorepati (KBC), 9 Aug. 2024.
109. Tata Group, https:// www.tatatrusts.org & https:// www.financial express.com 5 Feb. 2024.
110. D. Prakash Rao, "Asha Assawsana" Samaj Press, Buxar Area, Cuttack, Orissa, India, 2012.

www.ingramcontent.com/pod-product-compliance
Lightning Source LLC
LaVergne TN
LVHW041914070526
838199LV00051BA/2612